G. G. Urwin MA PHD

Brodie's Notes on George Eliot's

Middlemarch

D1612452

Pan Educational London and Sydney

First published by James Brodie Ltd
This edition published 1978 by Pan Books Ltd
Cavaye Place, London SW10 9PG
1 2 3 4 5 6 7 8 9
© G. G. Urwin 1978
ISBN 0 330 50133 X
Filmset in Great Britain by
Northumberland Press Ltd, Gateshead, Tyne and Wear
Printed and bound by
Richard Clay (The Chaucer Press) Ltd, Bungay, Suffolk

Contents

These Notes are based on the Pan Classics edition of *Middlemarch*, but as references are given to individual chapters the Notes may be used with any edition of the book.

To the student

A close reading of the set book is the student's primary task.
These Notes will help to increase your understanding and
appreciation of the book, and to stimulate *your own* thinking
about it: *they are in no way intended as a substitute* for a
thorough knowledge of the book.

The author

'George Eliot' was the pen-name used by Mary Ann Evans, who was born near Nuneaton in Warwickshire on 22 November 1819. Her father was the manager of Francis Newdigate's estate at Arbury Hall; almost immediately after her birth, the family moved to Griff House, the lovely and much loved scene of her early memories. A childhood spent in a district which was partly unspoilt agrricultural land following the traditions of centuries, and partly coal mines and quarries, had a tremendous influence on her later writings. Moreover, George Eliot's devotion to her father and elder brother can be realized by the characters she depicted. From an early age, she was clever at school, taking special interest in literature and foreign languages, including German, which was little studied at that time. When her mother died, she left school to take care of the house, but even then found time to continue her wide yet close studies.

As a young woman she was greatly attracted by religion, although she abandoned Christianity as a faith without denying the wonderful nature of its founder. Her first writing was a translation from the German of *The Life of Jesus*. When her father retired to Coventry, she went with him and stayed until his death. After that she found herself free to travel widely on the Continent.

After returning, she settled in London where she met John Chapman, editor of *The Westminster Review*, and fell in love with him; however, she managed to avoid becoming too involved with a man whose married life was already complicated enough. She contributed articles to his magazine and, in 1851, was appointed assistant editor. In London she enjoyed a varied and stimulating social life, participating in the intellectual and artistic events of the time and meeting many famous people, both English and foreign. But it was George Henry Lewes who made the greatest impression. He was a writer for magazines and a philosopher of considerable ability, but one who never achieved the fame he deserved. In 1853 he left his wife, whose private life was unconventional to say the least, and set up a home with Mary Ann Evans.

It was he who suggested that she should turn to fiction. Under the name of 'George Eliot' she wrote narrative-character sketches for *Blackwood's Magazine* in 1856; these were eventually collected as *Scenes of Clerical Life*. There was a great deal of speculation on the identity of the author, but only Charles Dickens seems to have guessed that it was a woman who was writing. The series was cut short, for George Eliot was eager to begin a full-length novel. This was *Adam Bede* (1859), to be followed by *The Mill on the Floss* (1860) and *Silas Marner* (1861). She and Lewes visited Florence; as a result, she felt the need to write about one of that city's greatest men, Savanarola.

However, *Romola* (1863) is a failure, for historical fiction was not her line. *Felix Holt the Radical* (1866) was a return to the setting and the style to which she was accustomed, though its basis is political rather than social – the Reform Bill of 1832.

In 1869 she began to write a story about Fred and Rosamond Vincy and the people they married, but evidently found difficulty in developing it. Then in November 1870 she put that story aside to begin a short work on a theme she had long considered – provincial life in its many forms, and the significance of ordinary lives. This was 'Miss Brooke'. In March 1871 she united the two unfinished pieces of work, and, with considerable difficulty because of illness and bereavement made them into *Middlemarch*. It was published by Blackwood in eight bi-monthly or monthly parts between December 1871 and December 1872. This method of publication naturally influenced the style and construction, but her skill in overcoming the difficulties of episodic writing was partly responsible for its being immediately accepted as her best novel.

George Eliot wrote one more book – *Daniel Deronda*, also issued in parts (1874–6). Her extremely happy relationship with Lewes ended only with his death in 1879. She desperately felt in need of someone to give her a devotion on which she had come to rely. Therefore she married John Walter Cross, twenty years younger but long an ardent admirer of her writing. However, she died a few months afterwards on 22 December 1880. She was buried next to the grave of G. H. Lewes.

George Eliot and contemporary novelists

1857 Scenes of Clerical Life
Little Dorrit (Dickens); *The Virginians* (Thackeray); *Barchester Towers* (Trollope); *Tom Brown's Schooldays* (Hughes); *The Professor* (Brontë).
1858 *Eric* (Farrar); *Dr Thorne* (Trollope).

1859 Adam Bede
A Tale of Two Cities (Dickens); *The Ordeal of Richard Feverel* (Meredith).

1860 The Mill on the Floss
Great Expectations (Dickens); *The Woman in White* (Collins).

1861 Silas Marner
The Cloister and the Hearth (Reade); *East Lynne* (Wood); *Framley Parsonage* (Trollope); *Ravenshoe* (H. Kingsley).
1862 *The Channings* (Wood); *Lady Audley's Secret* (Braddon).

1863 Romola
Hard Cash (Reade); *Salem Chapel* (Oliphant); *The Water Babies* (C. Kingsley); *Sylvia's Lovers* (Gaskell); *The Gladiators* (Whyte-Melville).
1864 *Our Mutual Friend* (Dickens); *Uncle Silas* (Le Fanu); *The Small House at Allington* (Trollope).
1865 *Alice in Wonderland* (Carroll).

1866 Felix Holt

Hereward the Wake (C. Kingsley).
1867 *The Last Chronicles of Barset* (Trollope).
1868 *The Moonstone* (Collins); *Under Two Flags* (Ouida);
Little·Women (Alcott)
1869 *Phineas Finn* (Trollope); *Lorna Doone* (Blackmore);
Puck (Ouida); *The Innocents Abroad* (Twain);
Good Wives (Alcott).

1871 Middlemarch

Through the Looking-Glass (Carroll).
1872 *Under the Greenwood Tree* (Hardy); *Erewhon* (Butler);
The Adventures of a Phaeton (Black); *Ready-Money Mortiboy*
(Besant & Rice).

1874 Daniel Deronda

Far from the Madding Crowd (Hardy).
1876 *Beauchamp's Career* (Meredith); *The American* (James);
Red as a Rose Is She (Broughton); *The Adventures of Tom Sawyer*
(Twain).

Plot construction

The reader must remember that *Middlemarch* was created out of two unfinished books, and that it was originally published in eight episodes. Owing to this serialization, George Eliot had to ensure that each section contained matter relating to most of the main plots and was left incomplete so as to stimulate interest in the next one.

The action of the novel may be sub-divided into eight distinct stories, though two are minor:

(a) Casaubon and Dorothea
(b) Ladislaw and Dorothea
(c) Lydgate and Rosamond
(d) Fred and Mary
(e) Lydgate and Bulstrode
(f) Bulstrode's past life
(g) Fred and Featherstone
(h) Brooke's political ventures

The author has shown great skill in interweaving these eight plots, which are linked by more means than there is room to mention here. In ensuring that the various parts of the action are closely related, George Eliot has depended on some coincidence that is not perhaps very credible; however, it is surprising how little there is and how rarely the reader finds it disturbing. Further details of plot will be found in the chapter summaries.

Inter-relation of characters

The intricate weaving together of the different stories provides one method of making the novel a compact unity: another method is to show comparisons and contrasts between characters so clearly that words and events frequently encourage the reader to recall previous episodes and aspects of character.

So many are the points of comparison and contrast that only a few can be detailed here. The reader should look for further relationships, and consider how they strengthen the structure of *Middlemarch*.

Dorothea and *Celia* as sisters: their different attitudes to Sir James: intellectual as against domestic interests: idealism against practicality: imagination and aspiration against contentment, even dullness: but also self-will against complaisance: the wife of a recluse and later a Londoner of importance against the wife of a locally important landowner.

Sir James Chettam and *Casaubon*. The open-air type of man as against the scholar: the practical landlord against the student lost in useless learning: physical health against illness.

Ladislaw, Lydgate and *Bulstrode* as people living in Middlemarch who have never been wholly accepted by the community because they were born outside it.

Ladislaw and *Fred Vincy* as men with good education: both are without careers and waste their talents: they apparently have little hope of gaining the women they love: eventually they make suitable careers: eventually, too, they marry the women concerned.

Dorothea and *Rosamond*: both young and attractive: both are eager to marry men considered unsuitable by their families: both make marriages which turn out unhappily: both lose money and status by them: both show interest in men other than their husbands. But their attitudes to their husbands and marriage are very different, as are the reasons for disobeying their husbands.

Rosamond and *Mary*, the sister and the future wife of Fred. Selfishness as against selflessness: desire for money and rank against willing suffering in menial occupations: the daughter of a seemingly prosperous manufacturer against the daughter of a bankrupt.

Casaubon and *Ladislaw*, the cousins. Wealth as against poverty: orthodox religion against a belief in beauty: the scholar against the artist: dull erudition against imagination: selfish desire to make use of Dorothea against unselfish desire to make her happy: coldness against passion. Each in his own way seeks to educate Dorothea.

Casaubon and *Brooke*. Each boring after his own manner: each muddle-headed: each a collector who has made no use of his acquisitions. But ceaseless devotion to one aim in life against lack of concentration and continual shift of interest.

Casaubon and *Lydgate*; both researchers, one in philosophy, the other in science: both fail, one owing to his incompetence and the other owing to unfortunate circumstances: both wish their wives to be little more than assistants to their careers.

Casaubon and *Farebrother*. Both waste their efforts on useless work, though for different reasons, the one on collecting books and manuscripts, the other on collecting insects: both are clergymen. Neglect of parish work against dutiful care of the parish: wealth against poverty: loneliness against a contented family of women relatives: married life with the woman of his choice against life as a disappointed bachelor.

Mrs Bulstrode and *Rosamond* as wives of humiliated men. Love against contempt: realization of the situation against utter refusal to consider any point of view but her own: deeper understanding of her husband against increasing incompatibility.

Bulstrode and *Fred.* Both aimed to establish their security on money left to them: the one gains a fortune, the other does not.

Chettam and *Brooke* as landlords. Sense of responsibility as against irresponsibility: regard for tenants' well-being against spasmodic interest in them: improvements to estate against concern only for rents. Yet the one preserves game and is therefore acting against his tenants' interests, whereas the other is not harsh against poachers. Eventually, Brooke sets about putting his estate in order.

Ladislaw and *Lydgate*. The one cannot gain the wife he wants, and the other has no great desire to marry and eventually regrets the marriage.

Ladislaw, Chettam and *Farebrother* as men who find that their love for women encounters many obstacles, not all of which are overcome.

Dagley and *Brooke*, the miserably poor tenant against the wealthy, self-satisfied landlord.

Dorothea and *Bulstrode* as wealthy people with money to bestow on others: their motives are entirely different. Both finance the hospital and Lydgate: both are prepared to advance money to Ladislaw: both give up their social position in Middlemarch: both eventually have to lead lives very different from those to which they are accustomed.

Rosamond, *Lydgate* and *Ladislaw*. She flirts with both, for different reasons and with different results. One can also consider her flirtation with Captain Lydgate.

Garth and *Fred*. The one is in love with his work on the land, the other is disgruntled at having to start on a career for which he has no enthusiasm. However, Fred too becomes a contented estate manager, trained by Garth.

Background and themes

Political background

At the period when the novel is set, 1830–2, parliamentary constituencies were still much what they had been for hundreds of years, and therefore many MPs were elected by towns which had dwindled into unimportance, or near extinction, and had very few voters. These were called rotten boroughs. Members representing the counties, still almost agricultural, were very much under the control of the landed gentry, men owning estates and drawing rent from tenant farmers. Those parts of England most important to the country's future, the recently developed industrial North and Midlands, had few MPs. Throughout the British Isles the voting system was chaotic, and by far the greater number of adult men – and, of course, all women – had no right to vote.

As often as not, the local landowners put forward a candidate to their liking, someone who could afford to be an MP without a salary, and then ensured that all voters dependent on or connected with them voted as instructed. Free gifts, especially liquor, were to be expected at election time, and downright bribery might well be used. In Chapter 38 one is told how Mr Giles had tried to win a Middle-march election, but lost despite spending £10,000 on bribes to the voters.

Candidates would go to the hustings (a platform in some public place) to address the crowd (Chapter 51); they would run the risk of considerable violence, for the crowd wanted rough entertainment and one's opponents made no pretence of observing fair play. Eventually the contest was decided by a show of hands by the few eligible voters who had appeared at the meeting.

To get rid of rotten boroughs and tiny constituencies, and to increase the number of voters, there was widespread demand for the reform of Parliament. Yet any reform measures would have to be passed by an unreformed parliament. In an atmosphere of political unrest and hopes for the future, the events of *Middlemarch* take place.

However, to clarify the situation it is necessary to go back a little in time to the reign of George IV who, before coming to the throne in 1820, had ruled as Prince Regent during the madness of his father. The political trouble to the forefront was the demand of Irish MPs that Roman Catholics should have the right to vote at elections and sit in Parliament, provided that they fulfilled all the other necessary qualifications. On the understanding that he would resist these demands to the utmost, the Duke of Wellington formed a Tory government in 1828; but he developed so great a fear of nationwide violence, even civil war, that he agreed to free the Catholics from these restrictions on their political activities.

Because of this drastic change in policy, the Tories' ablest man, Sir Robert Peel, left the government to become head of a 'rebel' group.

The emancipation of the Catholics and the weakness of the Tory party gave new force to demands for parliamentary reform which had existed for some time. Up and down the country, middle-class people formed political unions, organizations pledged to obtain a Parliament more representative of the nation. The Whigs, i.e. the party in opposition to the Tories, decided to make reform one of their aims, and took charge of the movement, with Lord Grey, Lord John Russell, Lord Melbourne and Lord Stanley as their leaders. It will be noticed that all these anti-Tory reformers were themselves men from noble families with considerable fortunes.

By November 1830, with the new King William IV on

the throne, Wellington had run into so much trouble that he resigned, and Lord Grey succeeded him as Prime Minister.

In March 1831 this government, with Lord John Russell as its chief spokesman on the subject, introduced a bill to redistribute parliamentary seats, taking them away from small towns and giving them to centres of large population, and to give the vote to every man in a borough who owned property worth £10 per annum. Even many of the county landowners were in favour of the Bill because the counties obtained more seats in Parliament, and the voting power given to tenant farmers actually increased the political power of their landlords.

However, in October 1831 the House of Lords rejected the Bill, largely because of the number of members who had been given titles by the late Tory government. So great was the discontent that Wellington, still a very influential adviser of the King, considered there was very real danger of civil war. To keep the peace, Lord Grey insisted that the Bill would have to become law, and he was ready to create more peers to gain the necessary majority in the House of Lords.

At this, the opponents of the Bill gave way, and the Reform Act, as it was called, became law in May 1832.

After this epoch-making decision, there followed a period of reform in many other spheres of national life. The most important measure was the Municipal Corporation Act of 1835 which liberalized the government of towns and enabled all ratepayers to vote at local elections.

During the early 1830s there was a pronounced trade slump which brought a train of bankruptcies among the middle classes, Garth's for instance, and unemployment for many industrial workers. This trade recession is mentioned on several occasions in *Middlemarch*, but the violence which accompanied it is shown in only a few vague references to rick burning, machine breaking and sheep stealing. These were often the only means of protest against the anti-reform party and the low wages and miserable conditions endured by those whose survival often depended on the character of the landlord or employer. One sees what misery Mr Brooke can bring even to a tenant farmer when he refuses to spend money on necessary upkeep and improvements.

Another revolution was taking place, though it is barely mentioned. It had nothing to do with Reform or politics. The economy of Middlemarch is partly based on cottage industry, whereby each family worked at home as a unit weaving cloth for some large-scale manufacturer, but it was then a dying method. Middlemarch was out of date, for centralized industrialism was rapidly becoming the only effective way of producing goods in quantity.

The arrival of the railway – incidentally an anachronism, for it is unlikely that the new transport would reach Middlemarch until the 1840s – is feared by the farm labourers, but it is proof that the reign of machinery has been established. The spirit of the new world is shown by Caleb Garth, who has felt the ecstasy of mechanization. (Chapter 24). 'The echoes of the great hammer where roof or keel were a-making, the signal-shouts of the workmen, the roar of the furnace, the thunder and plash of the engine, were a sublime music to him; the felling and lading of timber, and the huge trunk vibrating star-like in the distance along the highway, the crane at work on the wharf, the piled-up produce in warehouses, the precision and variety of muscular effort wherever exact work had to be turned out', these are evidence of 'the indispensable might of that myriad-headed, myriad-handed labour'.

In *Middlemarch* there is mention also of another power typical of the nineteenth century – the press. However, only the local papers are considered in any detail, and they are typical of the older sort; they are highly partisan, irresponsible in their statements, scurrilous towards their opponents. Little wonder that Ladislaw felt that he had lowered his dignity by becoming involved with the *Pioneer*. There was still a feeling of contempt for anyone who was concerned with newspapers, as Sir James Chettam proved when he excalimed, 'What a character for anybody with decent connections to show himself in!'

Class distinction in Middlemarch

Middlemarch is a manufacturing town in the Midlands, probably Coventry; it is growing steadily in size and importance, for in the suburbs one may still find an old, substantial farm such as that in which the Garths live. The inhabitants are very proud of belonging to the town, and suspicious of anyone who comes from outside it, especially from London which represents the gay life to Rosamond but to level-headed citizens of Middlemarch is the centre of 'empty bigwiggism and obstructive trickery'.

The countryside which closely enfolds the town may seem too idealized in Chapter 12, but it is an essential part of the environment, for the estates of the wealthy stretch for miles on the outskirts and contain the neighbouring villages. The novel is largely set in country houses which, though not great mansions by standards of that time, are vast by ours – Tipton Grange the Brooke house, Freshitt Hall of the Chettams, Stone Court which was Featherstone's and became Bulstrode's, and Lowick Manor to which Casaubon brought Dorothea. With their spacious rooms, luxurious furnishings collected over generations, and ever-available servants, they form a comfortable setting for very comfortable people. The owners of these houses would never consider themselves to be aristocrats, though the Chettams are baronets: they are landlords of moderate estates, drawing their rents from tenant farmers and, if they have good sense, putting some of their income back into the estates by improving housing conditions, experimenting with new agricultural methods and buying new machinery and stock.

For such people the survival and enlargement of the estates is all-important: wealth is still considered to be the possession of land. Sir James takes great satisfaction from knowing that, if Dorothea does not remarry, the Brooke estate will pass to his son; Casaubon is determined that his land will not come under the control of Ladislaw; there is considerable speculation about which branch of Featherstone's family will inherit Stone Court, especially as few of them are of the 'right type'.

These landowners control the election of MPs for the county, and sometimes themselves stand for Parliament. Many of them distrust the new ideas of the Whig party, and consider that looking after one's land is likely to do more good than meddling with the constitution of the country. Hence Sir James is greatly interested in Dorothea's plans for the improvement of his farm cottages, and strongly disapproves of Brooke's neglect of his estate – yet he is against the provisions of the Reform Bill; and Brooke wants some sort of compromise because he believes the political structure of England to be fundamentally satisfactory.

This is the county society, which acknowledges the existence of the wealthy industrial middle class, but treats it with a certain amount of patronage and will mix with it only when business or common politeness demands. Yet there is change in the air: social classes are changing, regrouping, intermingling, so that Mrs Cadwallader can lament (Chapter 10) the passing away of those days when 'there was a clearer distinction of ranks and a dimmer distinction of politics'. She also detests the rich Lowick farmers who are their own masters – 'monsters – farmers without landlords – one can't tell how to class them' (Chapter 34).

The middle classes and their dependent inferiors form a close community which knows everything about everyone and their antecedents; it suspects all who are not born and bred in Middlemarch – Lydgate, Ladislaw, even Bulstrode despite his years there as the leading banker; it has no sympathy for a lady who actually married a foreigner.

'The aroma of rank' is strong in this town society, and with rank is equated money or the ability to earn money. Social status is shown by the costliness of housekeeping, the sending of daughters to expensive private schools, and the dashing style of sons 'elated with their silver-headed whips and satin stocks'. If one ceases to make money, one is cast out of this society, as was Caleb Garth when his building speculation failed. People are growing cold towards Vincy, for it is common talk that his business is declining; and Lydgate realizes that he cannot face the disgrace of being sold up for his debts. Even though trade is bad, one is expected to make quick profits: the man who matters is the man with the gift for making money. Rigg, for example, sells Stone Court to obtain the capital he needs to start up a business; Bulstrode, once he had the widow's fortune, accumulated even greater wealth and became one of Middlemarch's outstanding citizens.

There are many grades within this middle-class society, all of which must be carefully observed, just as they themselves recognize the superiority of the landowning class. There is no resentment of class distinction: indeed it is respected highly, for everyone is interested in finding the means of raising himself above his present level. In the novel no one succeeds, except perhaps Garth, who recovers his former social position; and one may feel that Ladislaw's eventual political career gave him a position which could never be obtained in Middlemarch. Bulstrode purchases Stone Court for his retirement but can never take up residence, and Rosamond fails in her attempt to be closely connected with Sir Godwin and his family. To become a clergyman gave one the right to be considered genteel – one was paid without being connected with trade. Therefore Fred Vincy is sent to Oxford so that he may rise above the level of a manufacturer's family; he refuses to become a minister, and brings even further disgrace to his middle-class family by becoming a paid worker, albeit a well paid one. The reverse of the situation is personified by Mrs Cadwallader: she not only has an honoured position as the Vicar's wife but she comes of a landowning family and is therefore considered superior to the inhabitants of Middlemarch and the equal of the Chettams and Brookes; she strikes hard bargains with tradespeople because she has little money to spare, and yet this bargaining is looked on as indicative of her superior position and therefore worthy of respect.

Ladislaw does not fit into this society. He is a gentleman but a poor relation, an educated man but a 'foreigner' by Middlemarch standards, one of a landowning family but a mere journalist. Not only is he very self-conscious about this unsatisfactory social position; he sees it as an obstacle to his ever being acceptable to Dorothea. His only link with the class to which he should belong is Casaubon's patronage, and when that ends he has nothing to commend him. Dorothea's solution is to subsidize him with her share of the estate; Chettam's is to arrange for his appointment as a minor official in one of the colonies, where he can live like a gentleman at little cost and without embarrassment to himself or others.

Lydgate, too, is a misfit. He is an impoverished member of a landed family. He has received a sound education and yet has entered a profession which was still considered ungentlemanly. The course of life he pursues in Middlemarch is not that of a doctor but of a moneyed gentleman,

for he cannot believe he should lower what he considers to
be his rightful standard of living.

The Garth family had sunk out of Middlemarch society
because Garth's business had failed; even before the bank-
ruptcy, they were on only 'condescending terms' with the
Vincys and other 'old' manufacturing families. The Garths
plan to retrieve a position in middle-class society for at least
their eldest son, rather as the Vincys aim to raise Fred's
social status; young Garth is to be apprenticed to an engineer
and, as one of the new class of technologists, attain wealth
and respectability by means of railways and other mechani-
cal marvels.

Mr Garth himself must remain in the uneasy position of
being neither town nor county. He is the paid servant of
the landowners; and when he attains a position of great
trust he ranks with the doctors, Trumbull the auctioneer,
Chichely the coroner, Larcher the carrier in a big way of
business, and later Fred Vincy, as someone of importance
to the community yet lacking the prestige which comes of
being one's own master.

Then there are the vulgar people typified by Featherstone's
relations and tradesmen like Mawmsey the grocer (Chapter
51); how much inferior they are in behaviour, speech, interests
and general culture is nowhere more clearly illustrated than
in Chapters 32 and 35.

Mary Garth, reduced to earning a living as a governess,
has become 'brown, dull and resigned', and, of course,
respected by no employer. Very little pity was spared for
unmarried women who had to earn their own living.

Of those at the bottom of the social scale there is very
little information. One has a glimpse of the Green Dragon
and its billiard-room, the meeting place for shady characters who are interested in horses and consider themselves
sporting men. One meets for only a short time Dagley the
impoverished tenant farmer who is the victim of a bad

landlord. Some labourers are so discontented with their conditions that they burn hay- and corn-ricks, but most of them are apparently comfortable and satisfied: Dorothea found on enquiry (Chapter 9) 'not a cottager in those double cottages at a low rent but kept a pig, and the strips of garden at the back were well tended. The small boys wore excellent corduroy, the girls went out as tidy servants, or did a little straw-plaiting at home.'

Far different were the lives of those ragged urchins of Middlemarch whom Ladislaw befriended. However, the industrial poor, the men who worked in factories and shops and inside their own cottages, are scarcely mentioned. There are disreputable areas, for instance the slums of Houndsley and a place depressingly called Chalky Flats; one is told that tanning is carried out, and there is 'slow, heavy-shouldered industry' centred on the stone-pits and water mill at Frick; one learns that Vincy and others depend on the wretched handloom weavers of Tipton and Freshitt who, with their families, slave daily in their foul cottages (Chapter 34); Dorothea is proud of the fact that there are no weavers in *her* village of Lowick and therefore a higher and happier standard of living. Yet these same miserable handloom workers risk the severe penalties of the law by breaking machines which they think will deprive them of their pitiful existence. A little humour can be seen in their gossiping, foolish women, for an example of which one should read the accounts of Mrs Dollop and Nancy Nash.

Thus *Middlemarch* is a novel about wealthy people who are proud to have money, and have little interest in those without it. George Eliot could write sympathetically about the poorer members of society, as in *Felix Holt* and *Silas Marner*, but she had lived all her life in contact with the well-to-do middle classes both in town and country, and she accepted the class structure of the mid nineteenth century with wealth and security as its principal aims.

The nineteenth-century attitude towards women

In the first Book of *Middlemarch*, Dorothea stands out in contrast to her complaisant sister as a woman who is not content to accept the position which society expects her to occupy. This position was one of complete inferiority to men: men insisted that they were superior beings, and women generally saw little strange about this attitude. George Eliot ironically stated (Chapter 39) that men actually resented any sign of ability in women: 'A man is seldom ashamed of feeling that he cannot love a woman so well when he sees a certain greatness in her: nature having intended greatness for men.'

As if to emphasize the difference between the sexes, men assumed at times a rather amused tolerance of women's weaknesses, a patronizing interest in their views because these were sure to be of almost no value. 'Women were expected to have weak opinions; but the great safeguard of society and of domestic life was, that opinions were not acted on.' That is why, in the Prelude, George Eliot declares that the nineteenth century cannot hope to produce a second St Theresa. It is also in the Prelude that she herself seems to accept the situation: women display not competence but degrees of incompetence, i.e. some are less useless than others in their views and actions. Then in Chapter 9 George Eliot comments on the forthcoming marriage of Dorothea by saying, 'A woman dictates before marriage in order that she may have an appetite for submission afterwards,' and her tone is not ironical.

Mr Brooke is confident of the superiority of men – 'Your sex are not thinkers, you know' (Chapter 6), and 'There is a lightness about the feminine mind' (Chapter 7). Sir James Chettam, with whom Celia is in complete agreement, adopts much the same view when important matters are to be considered, though he is ready to consult Dorothea about a triviality like the rebuilding of labourers' cottages; when she refuses to take his advice about remarriage, he exclaims, 'Surely a woman is bound to ... listen to those who know the world better than she does' (Chapter 73). Casaubon looks only for the 'purely appreciative, unambitious abilities of her sex' (Chapter 29), and Lydgate dislikes having to make serious conversation with mere women because 'They are always wanting reasons, yet they are too ignorant to understand the merits of any question, and usually fall back on their moral sense to settle things after their own taste' (Chapter 10). Yet even Mrs Cadwallader supports the men's attitude, for she sees in their innate good sense the only means of making something valuable out of a woman's life – 'when a woman is not contradicted, she has no motive for obstinacy in her absurdities' (Chapter 6).

It is another woman, Mrs Vincy, who well sums up, in Chapter 11, the point of view that any sensible woman should have about men – 'Be thankful if they have good hearts. A woman must learn to put up with little things,' and presumably big things, too.

As George Eliot points out on a number of occasions, the belief in the essential flightiness and irresponsibility of the female sex was part of a vicious circle; they were educated on the assumption that they were empty-headed, they therefore learnt only what men considered was attractive in their womenfolk, and so when at last they joined adult society they could never be on a par with men. 'Struggling in the bands of a narrow teaching, hemmed in by a social life which seemed nothing but a labyrinth of petty courses', they eventually knew only how to make a man's leisure pleasant in a shallow way. 'A woman should be able to sit down and play you or sing you a good old English tune', is one attitude: another is Trumbull's (Chapter 32) – 'A man whose life is of any value should think of his wife as a nurse.'

The destiny of a woman is not to be clever but to ensure

that men are clever. In Chapter 27 Lydgate believes that it is 'one of the prettiest attitudes of the feminine mind to adore a man's pre-eminence without too precise a knowledge of what it consisted in'. Casaubon (Chapter 5) states very precisely, 'The great charm of your sex is its capability of an ardent self-sacrificing affection, and herein we see its fitness to round and complete the existence of our own'; and Dorothea herself claims (Chapter 4), 'I should wish to have a husband who was above me in judgement and in all knowledge'.

Young and old alike must find some means of filling in 'the gentlewoman's oppressive liberty' and 'busy ineffectiveness'. A few like Dorothea may perhaps seek activity in unrewarding academic studies; nearly all, the Rosamonds as well as the Celias, will base their activities on an education which encouraged them only in 'the combination of correct sentiments, music, dancing, drawing, elegant note-writing, private album for extracted verse, and perfect blonde loveliness, which made the irresistible woman for the doomed man of that date' (Chapter 27). More bluntly, (Chapter 17) woman had become 'the divine cow'.

Ironically, it is Lydgate, considering his own plight, who best sums up the unhappiness in store for a woman who dared to seek esteem for her intellectual powers: 'Only those who know the supremacy of the intellectual life . . . can understand the grief of one who falls from that serene activity into the absorbing soul-wasting struggle with worldly annoyances' (Chapter 73).

Equally ironically, though for different reasons, all three leading ladies in *Middlemarch* take the initiative when marriage is being considered; Rosamond, Dorothea and Mary cause men to propose when there seem to be good reasons for their not proposing. By the time the end of the novel is reached, all the women have accepted their expected situation in society. They are born to be married, not to exhibit intelligence; and there is no need to be ashamed of accepting men's prejudiced opinion, for 'Marriage ... is still the beginning of the home epic' (Finale) and, as Dorothea tells Ladislaw (Chapter 39), 'we are part of the divine power against evil – widening the skirts of light and making the struggle with darkness narrower'. By merely being women, they are the civilizing influence on society.

Religion and the clergy

Because *Middlemarch* is a study of provincial life in the early nineteenth century, it gives considerable space to religion and those who minister to it; however, it may be that George Eliot is unintentionally confusing the religious situation of her girlhood with what it was at the time of her writing the novel.

From a few scattered references, one detects an under-current of resentment against the Roman Catholics, for whose sake the Tory party had destroyed its political power; but apparently Middlemarch was little affected by the question of Catholic Emancipation (see p.15 on Political Background).

Nonconformist sects receive little attention and no respect. Methodism, which then had a strong hold on many parts of the Midlands, is referred to indirectly as a religion encouraging one to be dull and strait-laced. Dissenters – 'godly folk' – is a word used with a certain amount of disapproval and even contempt, for nonconformist congregations include dealers in stolen goods and the young, unscrupulous Bulstrode. They are loud in their profession of religion, critical of those who do not accept their view of life, outwardly respectable, and generally vulgar and utterly selfish hypocrites.

In Middlemarch, the Church of England is all-important. Yet, while life seems to move slowly by modern standards, there is a feeling of change in the air. The older generation, if Mrs Farebrother is typical of it, is much concerned (Chapter 17). 'When I was young ... We knew our catechism, and that was enough; we learned our creed and our duty. Every respectable Church person had the same opinions. But, now if you speak out of the Prayer-book itself, you are liable to be contradicted.'

What a range there is in the quality of the Anglican clergy, all of whom still live and work according to the centuries-old organization. They are all considered as gentlemen; they ought to have money of their own, as Casaubon has, and if they have not they must be content to live in genteel poverty, awaiting the award of some well-salaried post which may be bestowed as charity by one of the landowners. Dorothea, who has the privilege of nominating the Rector of the village, is perhaps unusual in giving careful consideration to the merits of various clergymen before she makes her choice.

One forgets that Casaubon is a clergyman because there is only one occasion when he showed some interest in his church, and then it was as a visitor. Since he has a personal fortune, he does next to no work in the parish, and does not even live in the official residence. Nobody considers this strange, or objects to his obtaining a comfortable sum of money every year for neglecting his spiritual work. He merely does what others in his position would do: he employs a curate to take full responsibility and then continues his life as a landowner and student.

Mr Tucker, the curate, is described in Chapter 9 as one of the 'inferior clergy', middle-aged and dull, rather seedy, not the sort of person one would wish to meet socially but 'doubtless an excellent man who would go to heaven', as Celia says. He is content with his inferiority, is seen but not heard unless required to speak, accepts his small salary, and is no doubt glad to live in the rectory.

Then there is Mr Tyke – the name itself suggests something rather uncouth – who has a minor curacy and needs to supplement his small income by taking the chaplaincy of the new hospital; he has some reputation as a preacher, but 'a good deal of his doctrine is a sort of pinching hard to make people uncomfortably aware of it' (Chapter 50). One learns of his virtues in Chapter 18, but he is little more than a superior servant of Bulstrode, dependent on his charity.

One can hardly think of such men being higher in social position than the Middlemarch manufacturers; yet even they were considered to deserve outward shows of respect from the most influential of middle-class laymen. Fred Vincy is being pushed into the Church – an uncle had been a minister – not because the family business is failing but because a clergyman gives an air of respectability and genteelness to all connected with him.

On a higher social level than these are Mr Thesiger the moderately Evangelical Vicar of St Peter's (Chapter 18) and Mr Cadwallader of Freshitt. The latter is an easygoing friend of all and never seems happier than when he is conversing with influential parishioners or fishing in a trout stream. Because he obstructs no one and can speak pleasantly on any subject that crops up, he is a very acceptable visitor and dinner guest. Besides, he is a 'High and Dry' Tory and is married to a lady of undoubted noble birth. Cadwallader does not take his parish duties very seriously, and nobody thinks the worse of him for being easy-going. Although he is the rector of Sir James's own church, his stipend is insufficient to allow of gracious living at his own expense; nevertheless, somehow he rubs along, a little shabby, short of luxuries, but greatly respected.

Farebrother, however, is not related to a family of importance; nor does his stipend provide comfort for his few dependants. Therefore he sees no harm in trying to win a few shillings at whist or applying for the post of hospital chap-

lain. Although he admits that he chose the wrong profession
when he entered the Church, George Eliot obviously considers him to be the best of the Middlemarch clergy: he
preaches convincingly – and she sets great store on this
ability; he works conscientiously and devotedly in the parish
of St Botolph's; he conducts his own life on the principles
he advocates from the pulpit, even to the extent of sacrific-
ing for another his hope of happiness with Mary Garth.
Therefore the author allows him to gain a monetary reward
in the shape of the well-paid rectorship of Lowick.

So much for the men who serve the spiritual needs of
Middlemarch. But George Eliot reveals a great deal about
the religious feeling of the times. There are a number of
references to the Low Church, a movement within the
Church of England which attached little importance to the
organization of the Church as a whole or to the mystical
significance of the sacrament; indeed, in many ways it came
close to the beliefs of such dissenting sects as the Methodists.

The Low Church movement with its liberal and reforming
views became associated with Evangelicism, about which
there is a great deal in *Middlemarch*. Assuming that all men
are corrupt but some are fortunate enough to receive God's
special grace and favour, it stresses the importance of intense
personal faith, and the application of one's own judgement
to moral issues; it encourages piety and earnestness and
thereby discourages any activity which may be called
frivolous or merely amusing; it seeks the reform of anti-
social practices and urges each individual to give himself up
to good works. Lydgate's judgement of Evangelicism is
biting: 'what is called being apostolic now, is an impatience
of everything in which the parson doesn't cut the principal
figure'. It seems typical of Middlemarch conservatism that
the inhabitants are still suspicious of Evangelicism, whereas
the movement was firmly established in many parts of the
country; however, as one reads in Chapter 17, it is gaining

ground to the dismay of even the more tolerant members
of the Church of England.

As George Eliot interprets the Evangelical movement, it
is illustrated at its best and its worst by Bulstrode's career.
In Chapter 16, for example, there are several instances of
his good works, the outcome of his strong religious beliefs.
On the other hand, they encourage his displays of intense
piety, his self-satisfaction, his scorn of those who do not
measure up to his standards of religion, his complete assur-
ance of his manner in dealing with everyone whom he considers to be inferior to him. As Mr Farebrother says in
Chapter 17, 'I don't like the set he belongs to: they are a
narrow ignorant set, and do more to make their neighbours
uncomfortable than to make them better. Their system is a
sort of worldly-spiritual cliqueism: they really look on the
rest of mankind as a doomed carcase which is to nourish
them for heaven.'

Evangelicism gives rise to Bulstrode's great pride, and his
fall is all the greater. We are told of his shame for misdeeds
committed long before: far stronger is his reaction to the
humiliation he has brought on himself by his assertive
religion.

George Eliot's own form of scepticism obviously colours her
attitude to the clergy and the churches in Middlemarch. As
if to emphasize her views, she not only states that the doctors,
including Lydgate, make no show of religious beliefs, but
that in the tribulations which dog Casaubon and Dorothea
they realize their faith is waning, and that Ladislaw's beliefs
are strongly tinged with an aestheticism more pagan than
Christian.

Doctors and the practice of medicine

In the 1830s, doctors were considered to be superior-type
tradesmen who had learnt the job as apprentices and then

made a living by dispensing and selling medicine. Lady
Chettam goes so far as to say, 'I like a medical man
more on a footing with the servants' (Chapter 10). Even
Lydgate, who had obtained as thorough a training as
possible by attending a number of excellent universities, had
begun his career as an apprentice apothecary (Chapter 15),
and his wife makes no secret of being ashamed of his
ungentlemanly profession. There was still no insistence on a
medical practitioner having qualifications, and when one
reads of the Middlemarch doctors, Toller, Gambit, Minchin
and Wrench (e.g. Chapters 18, 45, 63), one feels that an air
of respectability and a lack of any great religious conviction
were their best advertisement, 'the old-world association of
cleverness with the evil principle being still potent in the
minds even of lady patients'.

However, there are signs that the status of the profession
is slowly rising: the Apothecaries Act, mentioned in Chapter
15, to ensure some degree of competence in making up
medicines, had been passed in 1815, and doctors are agitating
for consideration as coroners because they are better qualified
for the work than lawyers (Chapter 16).

It is because Lydgate considers his work as a praiseworthy
vocation and is eager to participate in the new research
movements that he becomes unpopular with his fellow-
doctors who are satisfied with the old ways, and with the
inhabitants of Middlemarch who want treatment in the form
of medicine like 'squitchineal' and look on scientific investigation as something vile and ghoulish.

In the course of the novel there is a considerable number
of references to medical research of the time; Lydgate himself
is ahead of most of his contemporaries in that he uses a
stethoscope and knows the importance of post-mortem examinations. However, the advances made by individual
doctors pursuing their researches alone – as Lydgate intends
to do – reaches the rest of the profession very slowly. Indeed,

it is because his treatment of Raffles's illness is so novel (Chapter 69) that he feels sure that he will not be blamed when Raffles dies after his instructions have been ignored.

Although the new hospital plays an important part in *Middlemarch*, the reader never sees inside its wards. Its value to the novel is as an example of philanthropy, for institutions of this sort depended entirely on the generosity of local people. If the patron withdraws his support, the hospital may close. However, the fact that it is built illustrates the development of interest in providing medical care.

Lydgate's research deals partly with diseases of the heart, and he is called in when Casaubon has a seizure; but he is chiefly interested in the new lines of enquiry about germs and the nature of human tissue. At this period, germ diseases were the most prevalent owing to dirty, insanitary living conditions, and also they were the least understood. Vaccination against smallpox was still a fairly recent discovery; typhoid could be contracted by walking through the foul slums of Houndsley; cholera, which is mentioned on a number of occasions, reached England for the first time in 1831 and devastated thickly populated areas. A beneficial result of this visitation was the introduction by Parliament of legislation concerning the protection of public health. Bulstrode's disgrace (Chapter 71) occurs at a meeting called to consider plans for a new burial ground which may be required for future cholera victims.

The end of Lydgate's career is pathetic: he achieves financial security by doing what what he had always scorned: he abandons research and his high ambitions to improve the standing of general practitioners by becoming a fashionable physician, prescribing medicine to suit the whims of wealthy hypochondriacs.

Some other themes in the novel

Philanthropy

Before the 1830s there was very little attempt by any government to control conditions under which people lived and worked; indeed, any attempt by the State to interfere was viewed with great suspicion. Unfortunately, freedom to live and work one's own way was also freedom to suffer from unemployment, long hours, low wages, bad housing, impoverished old age, etc. Any reduction of these troubles was considered to be the responsibility of those lucky people with money to spare.

The urge to do good for less fortunate people was much in evidence during the period of reform, partly because living conditions for many had never been so bad as they were in the new industrial areas, partly because of the principles stressed by Evangelicism, partly because fortunes were being made rapidly and their makers felt some twinges of conscience.

Thus Bulstrode claims that he spent some of his ill-gotten money on people other than himself, unlike other well-to-do citizens of Middlemarch – who were also outwardly religious. His was the hospital which assisted both the bodies and the spirits of the needy; proud as he was of the power he wielded as the man in control, he erected the hospital for the good of the community.

Featherstone, to the chagrin of Fred, left the residue of his estate for the founding of almshouses. Did he do so chiefly to spite his detested relations? Brooke and Chettam, to different degrees and in different ways, seek means to improve living conditions on their estates, and yet their philanthropy adds to the value of their land and produces a bigger financial return.

Dorothea is the most outstanding philanthropist, as befits a lady with money. One would have expected Celia to be equally generous, but evidently she is content to enjoy her home life and leave good works to her husband. Dorothea is even rather disappointed that the villagers of Lowick are not in need of charity; still, she distributes flannel as required, organizes an infant school, and busies herself about improving the cottages on the estates of her uncle and Sir James.

She is ready with money to assist first Ladislaw and then Lydgate; she plans to establish a village community of industrious workpeople on lines suggestive of early socialist experiments, and to her comes Ladislaw with his scheme for a settlement, perhaps similar to the above or to Trawley's mentioned in Chapter 17, in the 'Far West'. These are all examples of good works considered suitable for wealthy people who were not connected with Evangelicism.

Yet one feels that all this philanthropy is a means of hiding one's true motives, or something separate from one's normal character. Even Dorothea is using philanthropy to fill in her leisure and, to some extent, quieten her conscience; and from her bestowal of charity springs a certain air of complacency and self-pride.

The Power of Money

Middlemarch deals almost entirely with the moneyed classes of the district, strict in the acceptance of a rigid class system based on possessions, and set against any change even when they have suffered by it. Life is largely a matter of every man for himself; if one is defeated, as were Garth and Lydgate, one must accept the reverse and find the means to regain one's position. Most of them could understand the need for philanthropy, but they saw no advantage in co-operation.

With money one can buy an estate or a seat in Parliament; one can obtain friends and keep the silence of one's enemies. Bulstrode personifies the power of money. He has used it to become an important banker and citizen, to obtain the Stone Court estate, to ease his conscience towards Ladislaw who had lost what he had gained, to keep Raffles out of the way, and to place Lydgate in such a position as to ensure his support.

In all fairness to Bulstrode, one must realize that all the other wealthy characters of note use the same power to maintain themselves in comfort – Casaubon with his vast library and protracted stay in Italy, Brooke with his excursion into politics, Chettam with his large estate and untroubled family life. Timothy Cooper says (Chapter 56), 'This is the big folk's world, this is', and the big folks enjoy the world because of their wealth.

And what do these affluent, influential people do with themselves apart from looking after their business interests? Very little, it seems, save for a little dog and horse racing, except return home for large meals and the enjoyment of their wine-cellars.

The women apparently spend most of their days visiting each other, holding tea and dinner parties, driving out to do good deeds, playing a little whist and passing on items of news or gossip. Mrs Garth is seen in her kitchen engaged in domestic tasks at the same time as she is educating her children, but she is forced by poverty to this mode of life. Her social superiors have servants to do all such work.

One sees them – Mrs Bulstrode, Mrs Vincy, Mrs Lydgate, Mrs Plymdale – sumptuously dressed, engaged in politely doing nothing. They live with their solid furniture, their jewels and silver plate, their pictures; but the impression which George Eliot gives is that they understand nothing of these acquisitions but the cost, and value them chiefly as symbols of their husband's earning power. They are the new Philistines, as Matthew Arnold termed them, and the author is not antagonistic to the attitude. To her, money is important and lack of money disastrous; this attitude is stated quite clearly in Chapter 64.

Lydgate's discontent was much harder to bear; it was the sense that there was a grand existence in thought and effective action lying around him, while his self was being narrowed into the miserable isolation of egoistic fears, and vulgar anxieties for events that might allay such fears. His troubles will perhaps appear miserably sordid, and beneath the attention of lofty persons who can know nothing of debt except on a magnificent scale. Doubtless they were sordid; and for the majority, who are not lofty, there is no escape from sordidness but by being free from money-craving, with all its base hopes and temptations, its watching for death, its hinted requests, its horse-dealer's desire to make bad work pass for good, its seeking for function which ought to be another's, its compulsion often to long for Luck in the shape of a wide calamity.

Frustrated Idealism

In some way or other, most of the major characters hope to achieve something worthwhile and deserving of their devotion; yet they fail, and must be satisfied with some other, perhaps less valuable achievement.

Dorothea seeks, through studying books and ministering to a scholar, some way of gaining satisfaction outside the narrow limits of household and children which usually restricted women. Yet she finds only disillusionment and sorrow, and in the end is eager to start afresh with Ladislaw on a basis of love and domesticity.

Lydgate is the new kind of doctor, enthusiastic about recent discoveries and filled with eagerness for research. He wants not only to use better means of healing the sick but to raise the standard of medicine and the reputation of doctors generally. Like his former friend in Paris, he finishes his career as a fashionable prescriber of medicines to wealthy invalids.

Casaubon, in his own strange way, pursued an ideal – the key to world mythology. The farther he went into the subject, the deeper grew his uncertainty; he began to doubt the value of his investigation, and died with his work unfinished – indeed, with almost nothing written. Moreover, his married life was a continual disenchantment with Dorothea whom he married to be his helper and admirer.

Farebrother had a stronger and more appreciative regard for Mary Garth than Fred could ever offer. That he never gained her love was partly his own fault – if self-sacrifice is a fault – but he had to accept a lifetime of bachelorhood knowing that he could never be more than a friend to Mary. Chettam, too, failed to gain the affection of a woman he greatly admired; in Book One of the novel it is Dorothea whom he hopes to marry, and it is largely the shock of her engagement that shifts his attention to Celia.

Rosamond has an overwhelming desire to leave Middlemarch and to mix with a society far superior to her own. For this she marries Lydgate with his gentlemanly manners and habits, and his highly acceptable relations. By her marriage she gains a brief glimpse into the humiliation of scandal, debt and lack of status in the town she so detests. In the Finale one learns that she eventually achieves something of her hopes, but at the expense of many forms of human happiness.

Fred Vincy at last gains what he had always set his heart on, Mary Garth, and he is a far happier person than Rosamond ever was; for all that, he has to surrender his hopes of fortune, social importance, even the respect of his own family.

The least saddening case of frustration is undoubtedly Brooke's. In his befuddled, casual way he eventually set his mind on becoming an MP, only to be laughed and pelted off the platform. He has not to suffer long, however; very quickly he readjusts himself and settles down on his estate.

Only Ladislaw achieves his goal. Perhaps he never hoped

for much, perhaps he is less selfish than any of the other characters, perhaps his ideals are more worthwhile than most – womanhood as personified by Dorothea, the beauty of great art, political reform. His life as described in the novel is a series of what seem setbacks and yet are advances towards the attainment of the apparently impossible.

The power of the past

The people of Middlemarch are shown to be conservative by nature: despite the changes which are affecting the country's way of life, they cling to old attitudes. When, reluctantly, they are forced to give way, they lament the better days that have gone.

George Eliot shows how, on the one hand, past events continue to affect the present; and on the other, that certain men attempt to regulate the actions of those who will live after them and yet fail to achieve their purpose.

The unscrupulous nature of Bulstrode's acts as a young man cannot be hidden, despite the lapse of years and the employment of large bribes. All the solid respectability based on wealth and religious observance collapses at the news of events twenty years old.

To this revelation is linked the story of Ladislaw's family. All his life he has had to suffer socially and emotionally because of the conduct of his mother and grandmother; and then his rather precarious position in Middlemarch and his relationship with Dorothea are endangered by information about the family's connection, long ago, with foreigners, the stage and criminals.

The past, in these cases, is a danger to the present. However, *deliberate* attempts to control future events fail. Casaubon plans that Dorothea shall finish his life's work, but she turns away from it in revulsion; he so phrases his will that she apparently cannot marry Ladislaw, but she chooses to defy his conditions, and to find love at the cost of the Casaubon inheritance.

Featherstone enjoys a grim game of playing one relation against another, each hoping to inherit a considerable part of the estate; in the end he is caught out by his own would-be cleverness and the last will is not destroyed. Thus his real intentions cannot be known for certain. And when Rigg obtains the Stone Court estate, as Featherstone apparently meant him to, he sells it without much delay.

Even Mr Brooke seeks to extend some control over future generations: his estate was to have passed to Dorothea's son, but he maintains that he will ensure it will never go to a son she may have by Ladislaw. However, because he is good at heart, or just too lazy to bother, he changes his mind and all is well.

The reward of virtue

George Eliot does not provide the conventional happy ending to *Middlemarch*; she was not a conventional writer, nor had any of her characters been 'good' in the conventional sense. Rather, people are rewarded when they learn to appreciate what is good in others and what are the weaknesses in their own personalities. Because of this knowledge, one can change one's way of life for the better, taking into account the limitations which save one from falling into self-pride. By knowing good and recognizing weakness, one is in a position to do good and achieve happiness.

The lives of Dorothea, Ladislaw, Fred, Bulstrode and possibly Lydgate, bear out this view; however, for the last two, knowledge comes almost too late and therefore their happiness is very limited. As for Mary, she seems to have had no illusions about herself from the first; she continues on her unselfish, balanced way, and the reader never doubts that she will gain her deserved reward.

On the other hand, Rosamond and Casaubon remain

selfish, petty, blind to reality throughout their lives, and never find any form of happiness; worse, they deliberately attempt to mar the happiness of others. In case one feels that Rosamond eventually gains some reward when she marries a second time, George Eliot shows that this marriage produces a form of satisfaction as shallow as Rosamond herself.

The sense of vocation

The Prelude to the novel states clearly what George Eliot believes to be the joy of following one's chosen vocation. 'Her flame . . . soared after some illimitable satisfaction, some object which would never justify weariness, which would reconcile self-despair with the rapturous consciousness of life beyond self.'

This is the feeling Casaubon no doubt had experienced, or hoped to experience when he began his researches into mythology, and which Dorothea fully expected to encounter when she became the pupil and ministering wife to him. Both believed that their vocation was philosophy based on academic learning; but Casaubon possessed neither the intelligence nor the imagination, and Dorothea had only the much belittled brain of a woman.

Lydgate's sense of vocation was not proved false; it was his tragedy that he became involved, not entirely by his own fault, in situations which destroyed any chance of his continuing the career he had visualized. Sad and disillusioned, he continued as a doctor, but the very sort of doctor he despised.

Most people consider that clergymen above all, should have a sense of purpose burning strongly within them. None of those who reside in Middlemarch or near it have the attitude of St Theresa which is explained in the Prelude. Farebrother honestly attempts to be a good parson although he is aware that he chose the wrong profession; Fred Vincy is ready to go into the Church despite his lack of interest or ability, for he can think of nothing better.

He is saved, and his future parishioners too, by Mary Garth and her father who understand the true nature of his abilities, as well they might, for the sense of vocation burns brightly in the Garth family. Caleb failed as a speculative builder, but he is a success as the manager of an estate. He loves the land and he loves machinery; he has a gift for understanding both men and animals. No task is too dull or lengthy or difficult if it is connected with his work. It is he who recognizes that this same attitude can be found in young Vincy, and therefore he trains him in the profession. Garth seems to have passed on the same spirit to his son, who is shown to have the makings of a dedicated engineer. Mary had no opportunity to feel dedicated to anything except the well-being of her parents; she has too many duties to perform. But she first insists that Fred must give up thoughts of a career in the Church and follow some responsible trade. So strong is her belief in the sense of vocation that she refuses to consider marriage with Fred until he abandons all thoughts of being a clergyman and finds a career to which he can devote himself.

Characters

Dorothea

'I have discerned in you an elevation of thought and a capability of devotedness.'

It is fairly obvious that Dorothea is in many ways George Eliot herself, with the addition of one quality about the lack of which she was always very conscious – beauty.

Dorothea is first seen as a young woman, glowing in health, fond of her comfortable life, and yet feeling somewhat guilty that she does enjoy it. She is highly religious – too religious for family comfort, Celia thinks – and ready to fly to extremes in her desire to find in life, and put into life, more than is expected of a well-bred heiress to £3,000 p.a. Hers is the spirit of sacrifice; it is recognized by Celia and by Casaubon – 'she likes giving up'.

But with this feeling of self-sacrifice goes a narrowness of understanding; 'I cannot help believing in glorious things in a blind sort of way,' she says in Chapter 22. Because Casaubon is so different from her foolish uncle and the conventional Sir James Chettam, she is fascinated by what she thinks is his profoundness of mind; she is fascinated by 'the great soul in a man's face' (Chapter 2) and 'a man who could understand the higher inward life' which she strives to attain. Captivated by the supposed spiritual and intellectual greatness of Casaubon, she has scarcely politeness for Chettam, who is not ashamed that his interests are those of a country squire.

When she informs Casaubon of her belief in the 'submergence of self in common with Divine perfection' and her 'soul-hunger' after matters of a 'theoretic' nature, his conversation leads her to think she has found the one person who can help her out of the narrowness and feebleness of a woman's world into the clear, invigorating atmosphere of man's intellectual existence. He will be able to teach her, inspire her by example, and raise her nearer to his great height by allowing her to take part in his ennobling work. She wants so much that a woman of her times cannot have, and yet she does not know what she wants; Celia's common sense leads her to say (Chapter 4), 'It is impossible to satisfy you; yet you never see what is quite plain'. And at this stage in her life Dorothea believes she can achieve some impossible ideal by study, painfully learning Latin, Greek and perhaps Hebrew, the everyday knowledge of a bookworm. Stubborn she is, too; Celia says quite outright (Chapter 9) that her sister is very impatient 'when people don't do and say just what you like', and Dorothea herself, preferring to call her stubbornness an independence of mind, admits (Chapter 54), 'I never called everything by the same name that all people but me did'. Therefore, despite the advice of all around her, she decides to seek her ideal by marrying Casaubon; she will organize her life in her own way, and in doing so one realizes that her high-flown idealism fails to disguise a good deal of childish naïvety.

It is at Rome (Chapter 20) that she realizes she is 'a mere victim of feeling'. A 'sort of mental shiver' passes through her as she experiences anger, revulsion, weariness, when she understands what she has brought on herself. In passing, one must remember that all illusions about her husband had been created by Dorothea, and she sees him now for what he always was and never pretended not to be.

Nevertheless, when she is made to understand how useless Casaubon's work is, and how different he is from Ladislaw, Dorothea feels not contempt or antagonism but the 'first stirrings of a pitying tenderness' (Chapter 21); so dull, loveless and hopeless is Casaubon's life that she reacts by suffering profound compassion. Indeed, she objects to the tone Ladislaw uses in telling her that her husband's work has been wasted. Lowick Manor will be a prison, but one in which she chooses to remain, for she must offer a lifetime of devotion to a man who will never show affection.

That her change of attitude towards Casaubon coincides with the arrival of Ladislaw is not given undue emphasis in the novel. Her delight in Ladislaw's company at this stage is entirely derived from his pleasant personality and his ability to discuss and instruct her on artistic matters that mean nothing to her husband; there is also innocent delight in the warmth and flattery of his words, for Casaubon can give neither. It may be appropriate here to mention George Eliot's dry remark (Chapter 29), 'If only a man could choose not only his wife but his wife's husband!'

Dorothea is angry at Casaubon's autocratic treatment of her because of Ladislaw's letters, but there is no doubt about her concern and distress when he is first taken ill. One remembers her loyalty when she first heard the truth about her husband's supposedly great work; and the realization of his wasted years only stirred a greater desire to be his help-mate and comforter. It is only in Chapter 40 that she grows incensed at his stubborn, jealous blindness and cries out, 'It is his fault, not mine'. Despite this, and the realization for the first time that Casaubon wishes he had never married her, she is eager to be reconciled, as one sees when she waits patiently in the hope of seeing him leave his late-night studies.

This generous nature of Dorothea colours so many of her actions. Her generosity to Ladislaw takes on a practical aspect, for she can bequeath him money as compensation for what he lost by his grandmother's unconventional be-haviour. She cannot believe that other people may be less generous, and therefore confidently expects that her husband will agree with the scheme. Warm-hearted, too, is her zeal in making life better for people in the district: she wants to play the part of the benevolent great lady, reforming conditions on the estates of Brooke and Chettam, financing whatever is good for the district, whether it is a hospital or a school bell; she wants to help Farebrother rid himself of his 'vices', to find work for Garth, to clear Lydgate's reputation, to repair the relationship of Lydgate and Rosamond.

All these activities are part of her nature, but they also serve as some consolation for the destruction of her hopes for intellectual development. She says (Chapter 39), 'I have no longings', for Casaubon has destroyed them; even her religious faith is declining; her friendship with Ladislaw is her one strong, personal form of happiness.

One can well excuse her embarrassment and annoyance at realizing how interested Ladislaw is in Rosamond. The fact that she suspects his motives (Chapter 43) and – much later in the book – thinks the worst when she meets them hand in hand (Chapter 77) shows that she suffers from jealousy that is not unexpected, and that her feeling for Ladislaw is warmer than she cares to admit. However, uneasy though she may be, she indignantly refuses to think ill of him because of the local gossip passed on via Sir James (Chapter 62).

However, Ladislaw and others are only side-issues; her main concern by far is Casaubon. 'She was always trying to be what her husband wished, and never able to repose on his delight in what she was' (Chapter 48).

It is ironical that when Casaubon at last seeks her assistance with his work, she feels compelled to refuse his demand that she will continue it after his death; she is still strong-willed enough to make a stand against tying herself down to what she does not understand. Out of sheer pity she will do anything to help him while he is living, but 'I could not submit my soul to yours, by working hopelessly at what I have no belief in' (Chapter 54), a statement which shows a more definite and spirited refusal.

How long she will maintain her independence she cannot tell, but it is obvious to the reader that she would have given way under hysteria and self-condemnation if Casaubon had not died. It is not clear, however, what her feelings towards Ladislaw are when her husband's will is known: she certainly yearns to see the young man and is desperate that she cannot allow him that share of her estate she had intended to give him. One thing the reader knows for sure: once Dorothea learns the restrictive, malicious nature of the will, any remnant of pity or respect for Casaubon disappears: she feels no obligation to honour the wishes of a man who tries to extend his jealousy beyond the grave.

The restrictions of the will are never likely to destroy Dorothea's attachment to Ladislaw; but it is he who must make the first move, and he considers that he must not. Thus both suffer an awkwardness and hurt which result in each saying what they wished unsaid, and failing to make any closer emotional contact. Just like Ladislaw, Dorothea has no thought of marriage. Then, when he tries to make her understand the nature of his devotion (Chapter 62) she misunderstands him: at last some inkling of the truth dawns on her, and she takes her carriage so as to catch up with him. But she merely passes by, such is her uncertainty. When she returns from her holiday in Yorkshire (Chapter 77) and grows melancholy at his absence, she still has no clearly formed thought of remarrying. It is the sudden shock of finding Ladislaw apparently holding Rosamond by the hand that brings on an emotional crisis. 'Oh, I did love him!' she cries when alone, but her reactions are anger, reproach, jealousy, all canalized into a compelling desire to help other people in *their* troubles.

When she learns the truth of Ladislaw's interview with Rosamond, she has the courage first to wring from him an admission of love and to make him understand that money is not essential to marriage, and then to defend her actions against the opinion of her relations, especially Sir James Chettam. Like Rosamond, she has taken the initiative to encourage a hesitant lover, and stubbornly holds to her decision; like Rosamond, too, she loses money and status by her marriage. But in Dorothea's case the loss is willingly incurred. Ironically, after such a series of unselfish acts she is accused by Celia of being utterly selfish in destroying the bonds which knit family and friends.

One's final impression is of a woman who needs love, or emotional appreciation of some sort, above everything else, and whose acts influence for good all she meets. She is a St Theresa of the nineteenth century, i.e. a woman who seeks to achieve what is denied to womankind. With nothing about her that is heroic, living in an environment that does not encourage 'ardent deeds', she has helped to make the lives of some people better and happier because of 'unhistoric acts'. As George Eliot writes in the Finale, 'Certainly those determining acts of her life were not beautiful. They were the mixed result of a young and noble impulse struggling amidst the conditions of an imperfect social state, in which great feelings will often take the aspect of error, and great faith the aspect of illusion. For there is no creature whose inward being is so strong that it is not greatly determined by what lies outside it.'

Casaubon

No better than a mummy.

As a young woman, George Eliot was fascinated by the father of a friend of hers, a Dr Brabant. He was over sixty years of age, a scholar, and – perhaps rather like Mr Brooke – something of a fool. She took on herself the role of a daughter, talking with him on learned subjects, reading to him, assisting with his books. At last Mrs Brabant objected, and the friendship was abruptly terminated. This episode in

George Eliot's life undoubtedly guided her when depicting Casaubon. However, while she was first considering the story that was to become *Middlemarch*, George Eliot became friendly with Mark Pattison and his wife. He was a lonely, embittered Oxford don whose life was devoted to studies that resulted in very little written work. Like Casaubon he was a clergyman who eventually lost his faith in Christianity; he, too, married a very young wife, charming and highly intelligent, whose life with him was most unhappy. Another link between the fictional character and the real person was Pattison's lengthy researches into the life and work of Isaac Casaubon, the Renaissance theologian and scholar.

The Rev Edward Casaubon is a middle-aged, sallow, dry student, and yet when the reader first meets him at the Brookes' dinner-table he is not entirely an unsympathetic figure, despite his silences and his over-precise remarks. His interests are wholly intellectual, and one is not told how valueless they are; his eyesight is failing, and one pities the state he is in. He is a man of honour, and one who has accustomed himself to severe self-restraint. Above all, to his detailed learning there seems to be a broad philosophic sweep whereby he can understand the interests, aspirations and emotions existing in other people: surely, one is led to believe, as is Dorothea, that he has those qualities which may be found only in great minds.

Yet no matter how pleasant the company of Dorothea may be, all he seeks from her as a wife is youthfulness to lighten his dullness and a willingness to act as reader, nurse and admiring audience. Our opinion of him sinks even lower when we read his cold letter proposing marriage; he is a prig, a snob, a man without affection, and therefore utterly selfish. Even his honeymoon must be arranged so that he may continue his work; and he is quite unable to understand why Celia should not go with them to occupy his wife's leisure time when he is engaged on matters more important than being companionable. To him the world is made for his convenience.

At Rome he is a 'rayless' figure lost in book-learning and fanciful theorizing, a man 'worn out on the way to great thoughts' that are never encountered. He is too languid to know delight and too narrow in his experience to understand people, therefore he appreciates neither his wife nor his famous surroundings. Above all he is afraid of reality.

It is during the honeymoon that Dorothea realizes his greatest weakness: he is afraid to begin writing his book lest he should reveal his failure to understand the subject. It is then, too, that another of his many failings is revealed — jealousy. Evidently the old man has enough emotion in him to resent beauty and youth — and intellectual achievements also. The visit to Naumann's studio (Chapter 22) suggests the first, and his views on his contemporaries (Chapter 29) suggest the second, though many other examples can be found. Along with this jealousy goes fear of everything outside his own limited experience and, most of all, of his own feebleness. In him is the growing fear that all his scholarship has been worthless, that his conclusions will be treated with contempt, that he is spending his life on something in which his interest is waning, that even his religious faith is slipping away. He is 'scholarly and uninspired, ambitious and timid, scrupulous and dim-sighted' (Chapter 29), 'nervously conscious that he was expected to manifest a powerful mind' and almost childishly delighted when his work receives praise. Casaubon retires further into himself to hide the truth from others, and he will accept nothing which suggests pity or sympathy for his failure. Therefore he is certain that Dorothea's devotion is 'a penitential expiating of unbelieving thoughts', and sees in her attempts to assist him the vices of rebelliousness, superiority, irritation and criticism. So, he cannot bring himself to begin writing and resents her urgings that he should make a start.

It is intense jealousy which dominates Casaubon's later days. And, ironically, it was encouraged by his misunderstanding of innocent acts – Ladislaw's letters to him and his wife, Ladislaw's stay at Middlemarch, Dorothea's visits to Lydgate, to mention only a few. It is not that he suspects his wife of being unfaithful; it is that he is certain she will become too interested in Ladislaw and *his* career, and will readily accept his views, that because she is a mere woman she will allow herself to be controlled by a man other than her husband. This lonely, uncertain, unhappy man seeks to maintain his self-importance by being the autocrat in his own house and insisting that his wife should be totally absorbed in his welfare. Casaubon's command that Ladislaw should not again enter Lowick Manor leads inevitably to his making a will that will keep the two young people apart.

Ironically, when at last he gains sufficient confidence in himself and Dorothea's intellectual ability to suggest her assistance with his studies, he antagonizes her by demanding promises which will tie her down to a life of pointless academic drudgery. How cruelly remorseless is the emotional pressure he exerts on her during the closing period of his life! He is determined to have his way, to make her accept his viewpoint as the only one. When he dies, he seems to have failed in his efforts to enslave her; however, by means of his will he seems to have maintained his authority and almost malicious influence. Yet ultimately, he has done nothing but strengthen Dorothea's repugnance and made firmer her resolve *not* to carry out his wishes.

Ladislaw

'Perhaps he has conscientious scruples founded on his own unfitness.'

Will Ladislaw is the poor relation who has been looked after and given a good education. Yet it has apparently been wasted on him for, as he himself admits (Chapter 21), he is amateur at everything. Lydgate, indeed, calls him (Chapter 43) 'rather miscellaneous and bric-à-brac'. Perhaps George Eliot visualized him as something like the Pre-Raphaelite painters of the 1860s, who were then looked upon with a certain contempt. Being what he is, Casaubon is prejudiced against Will, but he has some reason to be annoyed by his cousin's 'general inaccuracy and indisposition to thoroughness' (Chapter 9). Good-looking, charming, sensitive, well-mannered, but very touchy about his origins and his position as a dependant at Lowick Manor – such is Ladislaw at the beginning of the novel.

A new interest in Dorothea begins at Rome (Chapter 19), where he is sufficiently stirred as to become embarrassed and even jealous. He is quite unable to understand why she married Casaubon. There is never any suggestion that he wishes to take her from her husband; he detests Casaubon for denying happiness to his wife, and he himself seeks to provide that happiness by means of his attractive and knowledgeable conversation about poetry, music and art, the very matters about which Casaubon knows nothing. His beliefs that 'the best piety is to enjoy' (Chapter 22) and that religion is the love of whatever is good and beautiful (Chapter 39) show how different he is not only from Casaubon but Middlemarch society as a whole.

Meeting Dorothea encourages him to throw off his state of dependence; in future he will make his way by his own abilities. That this resolution takes him to Middlemarch – which he not infrequently decides to leave – is the result of a mixture of motives. First and foremost is the desire to protect Dorothea from the deadening life forced on her by Casaubon; then the friendship of Brooke gives him a weak but still useful link with Lowick Manor; and then he is offered paid work on the *Pioneer*, which gives rise to an interest in politics, possibly as a career.

At Middlemarch his relationship with Dorothea is much as it was at Rome, but more intense. His exposure of the futility of Casaubon's work (Chapter 27) is not to humiliate him in the eyes of his wife but to make her realize the truth of the situation in which she has placed herself and the waste of her young life in attempting to become the pupil and helper of a dull, unsuccessful scholar. He is ready to admit Casaubon's past generosity and his own difficult nature – 'I come of rebellious blood on both sides' – but he feels he must save Dorothea from a life that can offer no satisfaction of any sort. Certainly he has no thought of marrying her at Casaubon's death.

When Casaubon does die, Ladislaw is very conscious of his position, even before he learns of the provisions of the will. He feels keenly that he is a poor man, that he is socially inferior and of very dubious birth, that the local people are suspicious of him and will think the worst of him if he remains friendly with the widowed Dorothea. At heart he is convinced that he is socially superior to most people in Middlemarch. 'It ought to lie with a man's self that he is a gentleman', and therefore he will not accept Bulstrode's belated offer of an income (Chapter 61). Anything connected with his family's past damages his self-esteem and complicates his relationship with Dorothea, who, he is convinced, would be at least embarrassed if she knew the details. By being so thin-skinned and snobbish he causes himself tremendous anguish and prevents the natural development of Dorothea's interest in him.

Ladislaw's career in politics brings out a new side to him and gives him something he can to some extent enjoy. He is able to display his abilities in a practical manner: he has definite views which seem sensible, he writes to some effect in the *Pioneer*, he makes a good job of preparing Brooke's speeches, he does all possible to train his patron for the task of being an MP. That all these efforts come to nothing is not Ladislaw's fault. However, one knows that he is doing all this chiefly to be near Dorothea; despite his new feeling of importance, he is sensitive to the fact that by involving himself with journalism and politicians like Brooke he has lost his dignity as an intelligent being and a gentleman.

His friendship with Rosamond is ill-judged: he obtains from her company a certain pleasure which, because of circumstances, he cannot obtain from Dorothea; and he seems incapable of understanding the attitude which Lydgate and Dorothea herself might adopt towards what people would consider to be at least a flirtation. He claims to have no interest in Rosamond apart from her conversation and liking for music, but he rouses in her strong emotions and apparently never notices them. No wonder local gossip is so outspoken that Sir James Chettam is dismayed about its reflections on his sister-in-law. Then, even when he turns against Rosamond at the misinterpretation of his presence at her house (Chapters 77, 78) he cannot leave Middlemarch, for his friendship with her and Lydgate is all the more important since his relationship with Dorothea has become more embarrassing than before.

At one stage, Ladislaw is chiefly concerned with the idea of going away to make a fortune and thus becoming worthy of Dorothea's consideration. Even then marriage seems a long way from his thoughts. At last, in Chapter 62, he manages to overcome their mutual uncertainty to indicate something of his deep but long-suppressed affection, only to leave her feeling more hopeless than ever. He 'had seen heaven in a trance' but he expects nothing better. When, in Chapter 83, he and Dorothea at last learn the truth about each other's sentiments, Ladislaw does not dare to dream of a happy ending to his meeting with her; he is chiefly concerned with the need to confess the 'vulgar' nature of his parentage and to assure her that his own attitude towards her had always been honourable. Thus, as he talks of his love and the misunderstandings are brushed away, Ladislaw is obsessed with lack of money and lack of social standing. It is Dorothea who has to prove to him that they can live without wealth (though her own income is quite considerable), and it is his subsequent career in Parliament which gives him the solid, respectable position which he so needed.

Bulstrode

His soul had become more saturated with the belief that he did everything for God's sake, being indifferent to it for his own.

When Mr Bulstrode first appears, he is the great man of Middlemarch town, though still considered as a newcomer and a 'foreigner'. He has many enemies, even among his acquaintances, for not the least of his vices is his determination to override any opinion with which he does not agree; he has little respect for his brother-in-law Vincy, for, to the banker, money alone matters and the Vincy business is declining. Later (Chapter 40), Lydgate tells Dorothea that 'Half the town would take trouble for the sake of thwarting him'.

Because of his high social position, Bulstrode has no need to keep quiet about his opinions, and does not. He thinks little of the local doctors and clergy, he despises Fred and Rosamond because they are spoilt and idle, he treats the tradesmen as inferior and unintelligent accessories to his power. And it must be admitted that his attitude to these people is not entirely unjustified; besides, he recognizes efficiency and zeal when he comes across those qualities, and he is ready to spend money to assist both the community and individuals.

Whatever he does is inspired by his Evangelical religion. As a result he has achieved the reputation of being a hypocrite and a bigot. Vincy well sums up his character when he claims (Chapter 13) that 'one worldliness is a little bit honester than others', and then says that Bulstrode wants 'to play bishop and banker everywhere' and 'must be first chop in heaven'. However, nothing can shake the banker's confidence in himself.

To see Bulstrode at the meeting about the appointment of a hospital chaplain (Chapter 18) is to understand how appropriate is his name. Thus, to stress the tragic changes that have occurred, George Eliot shows him at the last meeting he attends (Chapter 71), when he is a discredited, sick man, no longer the domineering lord of the committee-room but the expelled member sneered at by all.

It is at the height of his power and arrogance, just when he has bought the *Pioneer* and taken over Stone Court for his retirement as a symbol of his wealth and social position, that his disreputable past is revealed. The events of thirty years before show that his religion and moral scruples are mere expedients; although he proves that he has used some of his money for purposes of good, the fact remains he had originally made his way by deceit and crime, and has since then been satisfied to pay for the silence which hid them.

What one learns of his early days (Chapter 61) is highly disreputable. He was an ambitious social climber – a counter-jumper – whose intense Calvinistic beliefs convinced him that God intended him for some special task and that anything was permissible if he could prove to himself that his actions accorded with his principles. Bulstrode had in-gratiated himself with Mr Dunkirk, the richest and most influential member of the congregation, and was later prepared to marry an old woman because she had the wealth which could be used for what he considered to be God's (i.e. Bulstrode's) purpose. He even satisfied himself that God would not want the money to be wasted on a runaway daughter and her dubious husband. George Eliot insists that he is not a bad man, rather he is one 'whose desires had been stronger than his theoretic beliefs, and who had gradually explained the gratification of his desires into satisfactory agreement with those beliefs. If this be hypocrisy, it is a process which shows itself occasionally in us all.'

Thirty years later, and only because the past is likely to be revealed, he is overwhelmed with shame, and feels a 'new spiritual need'. Yet how grudgingly he admits to Ladislaw as much information as he feels compelled to disclose, and how put out he is when Ladislaw does not accept his apologies and compensation. So long as Bulstrode can cling to some remnant of his self-pride, he does. And his own troubles do not make him at all sympathetic towards the plight of Lydgate his protégé; no money is to be obtained from him, not until the doctor has information which the banker wants to be suppressed. Equally reluctant is Bulstrode to face the fact that Raffles is a menace to his respectable life; always he believes that perhaps some way, no doubt concerned with money, will be found to preserve the secrets of the past.

When Bulstrode finds Raffles alone and ill at Stone Court, he is again faced with a dilemma which tests the genuineness of his moral principles. He wants Raffles to die, because death seems to offer the perfect solution to the problem. One wonders how long Bulstrode would have resisted the temptation to cause Raffles's death, and by what tricks of reasoning he would have convinced himself that it was right to murder him. However, he is spared this greatest of decisions, for Raffles dies as a result of Mrs Abel's innocent mishandling. Bulstrode convinces himself that he has *done* no wrong: he has merely allowed – perhaps encouraged – someone else to do what she and many doctors consider best for a patient in this plight. The £1,000 he pays Lydgate is not a bribe, so Bulstrode proves to himself, but a loan only recently requested by the doctor and recommended by Mrs Bulstrode. For all that, he cannot deny that he prayed Raffles would die.

Had Bulstrode left Middlemarch for nothing more than a prolonged holiday he might have lived down the scandal, for his wealth was important to the town. Instead, he delays his departure and mistakenly believes that his personality and status are still powerful enough to override the malice of his enemies. Therefore he finds himself humiliated in public, and addressed by Hawley (Chapter 71) in terms which have always been at the back of people's minds – 'ambitious', a man of 'self-preserving will', 'canting palavering Christianity', a 'saintly kill-joy'. The hatred of Middlemarch is poured down on Bulstrode the interloper, bigot and hypocrite. Even then he has enough spirit to insist that he has done more good with his money than have his enemies; they are no better than he but they have not been found out in their sins.

What stands most highly to his credit is his devotion to his wife, and his readiness to consult her wishes. He is persuaded by her (Chapter 14) to assist Fred out of the difficult situation created by Featherstone, and he is partly influenced by her when he assists Lydgate. Naturally, he has told her nothing about his early life, but it is not just shame that advises him to calm her fears with lies about Raffles and his visits. He cannot tell her the truth when the truth is about to be revealed by others, for he cannot bear her to suffer. It is Mrs Bulstrode who eventually goes to him and offers silent pity. Then, at the lowest point of his despair, he most deeply feels love for the woman he has deceived so long. The reader can derive some consolation from knowing that mutual affection makes Bulstrode's nature look less shabby.

The last glimpse one has of him is when he is overwhelmed with grief not so much for himself now but for his wife and the anguish, shame and feeling of isolation that she must endure. He is leaving Middlemarch quietly, unobtrusively trying to do some good by his departure, and chiefly intent on providing some comfort and peace of mind for his wife.

Lydgate

He had a profession and was clever, as well as sufficiently handsome.

As a doctor Lydgate has been considered elsewhere in this book (p.32). Here he must be considered as a man faced with dilemmas and emotional crises which are more obviously disastrous than those affecting any other character.

He is young, at the beginning of his career, and likely to lead a worthwhile life. Like Ladislaw he is a gentleman by nature who has reached his present position partly by the kindness of others. Now that he is independent he cannot adjust himself to the level of society suited to his profession, and his vague connection with wealthy relations encourages the people of Middlemarch to accept him for what he thinks he is, a man with money and good breeding. To give him his due, he finds the seclusion and calm of medical research more to his taste than the gatherings to which he is invited; and if he had only kept out of emotional complications he might well have been content to be a social attraction only when he found it convenient.

When one hears of his history (Chapter 15) one has reason to admire a man who has experienced difficult times and learnt his profession the hard way. He is no genius, but he is always willing to learn and he has an enthusiasm for new ideas in medicine, which gives him the air of a pioneer. Unfortunately, his 'conceit was of the arrogant sort'; his outspoken, tactless comments serve only to increase the prejudice against him, and there is reason enough to believe that, in his own fashion, he is as narrow-minded and opinionated as any of his colleagues.

Should he be pitied for his entanglement with Rosamond?

He has sense enough to realize that he cannot marry for years, and honesty enough to admit that he is quite satisfied with life as it is. Nevertheless, he is ready to use Rosamond's company as a diversion: sheer conceit more than anything else encourages him to carry on a flirtation without any sense of responsibility or thought for her feelings; even Mrs Bulstrode's words (Chapter 31) at first stimulate rather than discourage him. When he tries to restrain himself, and calls on the Vincys only professionally, it is too late, for he has brought about a situation that he cannot control. Nor can he understand the truth of it; Rosamond's chagrin is interpreted as the unhappiness of a bewildered child, the over-emotionalism of the moment as the passion of love.

It is easy to be hard on Lydgate, but he is not altogether a self-centred man. Priggish as he is to look askance at Farebrother's ungentlemanly interest in money, he does not oppose the Vicar's appointment as hospital chaplain because of that 'weakness'. Nor does he humiliate himself to keep in Bulstrode's good books: he seeks only to ensure that he will become superintendent of the hospital where he can do good to people and put into practice the theories in which he believes so strongly. He will be paid for his work, but he *is* working.

Yet he is partly the architect of his own ruin. Before he shows that he cannot manage Rosamond and her extravagance his fortunes are failing. He never considers any standard of living below that of a gentleman and sets himself up on the rickety basis of credit; he despises the family into which he has married, and considers his wife chiefly as a woman who will assist him to obtain the calmness of mind he requires for his research. Except for his zeal to reform medicine, he is a man who 'walked by hereditary habit; half from that personal pride and unreflecting egoism which I have already called commonness, and half from that naïvety which belongs to pre-occupation with favourite ideas'. In other words, he is at heart much the same as Sir Godwin Lydgate and Captain Lydgate, but he has almost no money.

Once married, he finds himself sinking deeper and deeper into disaster. Unpopular in the town, disappointing to his wife, closely linked to the much-disliked Bulstrode, always lacking money – this is the state from which he must drag himself unaided.

He quickly comes to understand that he can expect nothing from his wife Rosamond. He sees no harm in Ladislaw's visits to her, but he suffers badly from jealousy and a sense of inferiority when she openly flirts with Captain Lydgate. Besides, his authority is flouted, and he knows there is no means of exerting it over her. By this time, any love he felt for her has gone: he is aware only of her extravagance and stubborn wilfulness, and his own mounting debts for which she is largely responsible. Because of these debts he becomes obsessed with his wasted efforts, degradation and failure; and the wife with whom he is forced to live is the personification of discontent and irresponsibility. He feels utterly hopeless of ever being able to explain the nature of his predicament. 'I am at the mercy of your devices,' he tells her (Chapter 65) and in despair throws up his hands at defeat by 'an animal of another and feebler species'. George Eliot cannot resist pointing out the difference between Farebrother who renounced his chance of marriage to a woman he greatly loved, and Lydgate who would have done anything to put an end to marriage with a woman who constantly irritated him.

Matters are made worse because Lydgate is inclined by nature to keep his troubles private. Rosamond's ungenerous, unsympathetic attitude drives him more into himself; by the time of the Bulstrode scandal (Chapter 76) there has developed between them a situation comparable with that which once existed between Casaubon and Dorothea. 'I ought to be more open,' says Lydgate, but Rosamond discourages any sort of frankness.

Lydgate lowers himself in the Green Dragon

The episode at the Green Dragon does not seem typical of Lydgate. By his gambling there he puts himself on the level of the unreformed Fred Vincy and his disreputable acquaintances. However, the game of billiards illustrates the lengths to which he has been driven by debt and a foolish wife.

When he is called to attend Raffles during his last illness, Lydgate at first admires the care and tenderness apparently shown by Bulstrode, but before long he has a vague feeling that he is being victimized. Yet he does not suspect foul play, nor does he question too deeply the banker's unexpected generosity. When he has to decide on the rights and wrongs of the situation brought about by the revelation of Raffles's secret, he supports Bulstrode in public and refuses to be ashamed at taking the money. Is he trying to deceive himself into believing his own innocence or does he genuinely feel that he is clear of any mistake or wrongdoing? The only person capable of giving the necessary strength and confidence needed to face the aftermath of the scandal is not his wife but Dorothea.

In the Finale one learns that Lydgate has come to terms with life; to remain a 'gentleman' he has thrown aside his pride in being a doctor, to gain money he has accepted the patronage of wealthy invalids whom he probably despises, and to find some means of living peaceably with Rosamond he learns to accept her with 'sad resignation'.

Rosamond

She cared about what were considered refinements, and not about the money that was to pay for them.

From the first, Rosamond is presented as a self-centred product of a ladies' academy, the spoilt daughter of a complacent, wealthy family. Yet, spoilt as she is, she is thoroughly discontented with the narrow, dull life of Middlemarch; eager young men – quite good candidates for marriage, all of them – are treated with contempt, and her heart is set on getting away to London.

Thus the arrival of a gentleman-doctor is something in itself to rouse her selfish interest; far more important is his connection with an aristocratic family. Marriage to Lydgate, therefore, is merely her means of escaping from an environment unsuited to her supposedly superior talents to a life of social importance.

Rosamond sets out to entrance Lydgate by putting on something of an air of a naïve provincial girl overwhelmed by his urbane charms, and by showing off her petty accomplishments. Then, when her brother Fred's illness accidentally brings together Lydgate and her, she goes out of her way to intensify the attraction which she exerts on him. How ironical it is, therefore, that she is staying at Stone Court so as to prevent Fred from succumbing to the charms of Mary Garth, who is considered vulgar by Vincy standards.

As Lydgate intends to go no further than a flirtation with her, one can perhaps sympathize with Rosamond; on the other hand, the difficult situation in which she finds herself is caused by the selfishness of two people interested only in gaining their own ends. How far she is genuinely embarrassed and mortified by Lydgate's stiff and formal attitude to her when he decides to keep clear of any entanglement, and how far she consciously brings about the emotional situation which forces Lydgate into proposing, the reader must decide for himself from his interpretation of Chapter 31 and the events leading up to it. In view of what happens later in the novel, it should be remembered that, from the first, Rosamond had set her mind on marrying Lydgate.

Once she is engaged, she is clearly seen to be what Mrs Bulstrode thought she was, extravagant, an utter snob and stubborn in the extreme. She will not be budged from her plans, not even by her father, who is far from happy about the proposed marriage.

Rosamond's attitude to the other man of importance to her, Ladislaw, is not what he imagined it to be. He wanted companionship, a pleasant listener, someone to dispense domestic comfort whenever he called; she saw him as the opposite of a husband with whom she has quickly been disillusioned. Although she is convinced that he is much fonder of Dorothea than he admits, she is obviously prepared to encourage the development between them of a strongly emotional feeling. She always has needed the company of men in order to show herself off, and later (Chapter 75) she needs flirtation with Ladislaw to compensate for her lack of love for her husband.

She will go further with Captain Lydgate: her open delight in the 'superior' ways of this unscrupulous lady-killer leads her to defiance of her husband's advice and commands; so determined is she to have her own way and indulge her whims that she has an accident resulting in a miscarriage, and still she blames her husband. The jealousy which seems to be roused in Lydgate quite pleases Rosamond, for she sees it as a tribute to her womanhood and personal charm.

The picture of her in Chapter 58 is frightening, as Lydgate knows. The 'terrible tenacity of this mild creature' is clearly shown; her inability to accept reality, her extravagance which she insists on almost as a right, her demands that all opinions must agree with hers or else be wrong, her air of martyrdom and cold disdain if she does not get her own way. As Lydgate's troubles increase, so does Rosamond's lack of concern for them. She becomes, more than ever, a figure of affronted dignity, confident in other people's desire to rush to her assistance, and contemptuous of all that does not measure up to her standards. And everyone is judged by an adamant, unforgiving nature.

Having destroyed Lydgate's affection, she seems ready to destroy the bond between Ladislaw and Dorothea. Despite her husband's instructions, she tells Ladislaw about the provisions of Casaubon's will; when he is stung by circumstances (Chapter 78) to tell her of his love for Dorothea, she is pained as she had never been by anything of Lydgate's doing. Selfish in everything, she does not intend to leave her husband or even to deceive him, but she wants to keep other men all for herself as admiring courtiers.

Can one accept the sudden impulse to do good in Chapter 81 or is this a move engineered by George Eliot and quite out of character? For what is it that makes Rosamond disclose to Dorothea the nature of Ladislaw's visit to her, and thereby open the way for his marriage to the only woman he loves? To some extent it is nervous strain caused by months of ever-increasing financial and domestic troubles, the highly emotional state encouraged by Dorothea's own passion and sorrow, and the pressure Dorothea exerts owing to her urge to help a fellow-woman in trouble. For the only time in her life Rosamond does good, knowing that she herself will suffer. The impulse to tell the truth and clear away misunderstandings does not last long: the note she writes to Ladislaw informing him that she has told Dorothea what really happened during his visit is not a generous gesture by someone who likes him; it is the cold dismissal from life of a man who can no longer be useful or entertaining.

By having insufficient money, Lydgate has proved useless to her; and when disaster falls on him, she is useless as a wife. She is cold and antagonistic, affected only by shame and mortification at the prospect of having to lower her standard of living. The only practical moves she makes are obstructive and in flagrant disregard of her husband's wishes. She is determined to frustrate anything which she views with disapproval. Against her 'quiet elusive obstinacy' Lydgate can do nothing. She turns to her own family, to Sir Godwin Lydgate, to Ladislaw, but never to her husband; and nothing will ever convince her that she has in any way been unsympathetic or disloyal. There falls between them a silence but not the silence of mutual understanding.

She gets what she wants, comparative affluence, a life far away from Middlemarch, and a circle of fashionable acquaintances. In return she maintains the convention of fidelity to her husband; she certainly cannot give love. The latter part of her relationship with Lydgate is nothing but a pain to be borne, and she looks on her second marriage, equally loveless, as a 'reward' for years of tolerating Lydgate.

Fred Vincy

A spirited young fellow, with a good appetite for the best of everything.

In rather patronizing tones George Eliot thoroughly reviews Fred's character in Chapter 23. Like Rosamond, for whom he has no affection, he is the pampered, selfish child of irresponsible parents. All he cares for is the continuation of an easy-going life, with the addition of Mary Garth as a wife. Work at the university bores him, the thought of becoming a minister appals him. As he himself says (Chapter 14). 'I should not have made a bad fellow if I had been rich.' Unfortunately, the family fortunes are running down.

With all the optimism of a spoilt child and the conceit that comes of inexperience, he bases his plans for the future on receiving a fortune from the old man at Stone Court. That he should involve innocent people in his financial difficulties does not seem wrong to him, nor does his betrayal of a trusting friend already facing troubles enough, Caleb Garth. Fred cannot see beyond his own need for money and the likelihood of money being found somehow. When he has to reveal the disastrous situation in which the Garths are placed, he feels shame at his own predicament rather than any understanding of the hardships he has caused.

Though he is uninfluenced by Mrs Vincy's snobbish

opinion of Mary Garth, Fred at first experiences love chiefly
as a result of his selfishness. He has always known Mary
and therefore she should marry him; he ought to turn away
from his bad habits and therefore Mary must help him
for he himself cannot. He even feels hurt when she refuses
to have him as he is. Full of self-pity and embarrassment
at his misfortunes, he goes off to see Mary (Chapter 25) and
is quite annoyed when she at first offers no consolation. He
even accuses *her* of being selfish. When she does try to show
sympathy for his failure to obtain the Featherstone money,
he becomes quite violent in his chagrin and self-pity: all he
can understand is that he must lower his standard of living
and work hard to obtain a start in a career he dislikes.

When Fred returns from university with a degree, he is a
quieter and a chastened man, more devoted to Mary but less
certain of his chances with her. He obviously cannot
understand her scruples about his choice of a profession.
Being a parson, to him, is a means of obtaining money and
being a gentleman, unattractive as the work may be.

After Fred, by accident, has taken up a practical type of
business – as Mary always knew he should – he is a far
pleasanter person. He is quite attractive in his rather childish
attitude towards making a living – his enthusiasm can easily
wane if it is not constantly encouraged, he expects im-
mediate success, he reveals for a time his sheer inability
despite all his education, he slips away whenever he can
from the discipline of work.

Nevertheless, he grows into a decent man, not completely
successful but one who can take pride in himself, his family
and his work. It seems obvious that the force behind him is
his wife Mary, but he has in himself the virtues that make
'not . . . a bad fellow' although he is not rich. Having come
to know himself and his limitations he obtains the happiness
he deserves.

Mary Garth

She neither tried to create illusions, nor indulged in them for her own behoof.

When she is introduced in Chapter 12, Mary is explicitly shown to be imperfect; yet she has, among other excellent qualities, something that even Dorothea seems to lack – common-sense. Even fuller is the picture of her in Chapter 40, and there again her faults are revealed. Nevertheless, the over-all impression is that she is the most level-headed, highly-principled person in the novel. She is not in a position to have the over-confidence and conceit of some other characters, for she must earn her own living as a governess or companion. However, she has a 'streak of satiric bitterness' as well as a praiseworthy 'honesty, truth-telling fairness', and that bitterness is encouraged by the very man she loves, Fred Vincy.

In days when marriage was so important, especially to an impoverished woman, Mary refuses to consider it except on her own terms; she will not tolerate a man for whom she feels contempt, and insists that he should raise himself to her standards. She says that *she* cannot change him. She does not want to change his character; her duty is to encourage him to make the change himself and to develop 'manly independence'. Despite this contempt for the waster Fred, she shows no great resentment when he involves her family in ruin by his horse-dealing, and is dutifully ready to hand over her meagre savings to help pay his debts.

One is shown, too, her devoted service to Featherstone without any thought of reward. Despite his ill-temper, sarcasm and irritating whims, she patiently goes about her tasks. On his death-bed it is her determination to do what she knows is right and her consideration for the old man that bring about the downfall of Fred's hopes for a fortune and, consequently, for marriage.

She would never have married him if he had obtained Featherstone's money, but her love for him would have remained. She is honest enough to despise his weaknesses but her love is somehow unaffected. Sad as she is at doing so, she has no hesitation in refusing the timid advances of Farebrother, whom she greatly admires both as a man and as a clergyman. But neither does she hesitate in refusing Fred when he returns from university with the prospect of a satisfactory career; she will not marry him while he seeks 'imbecile gentility' in the Church without any principles or sense of vocation. She unashamedly wants Fred, she wants to reward his years of devotion, but it must be the kind of Fred she knows to be the true one.

When Fred has embarked on a new, practical career and can take some pride in himself, she is so eager to show her happiness that she takes the initiative and brings about their marriage. Altogether, Mary Garth is a very unconventional young lady, and a good deal of the unconventionality springs from her having strict principles which she is not ashamed to own.

Chettam, Brooke and Garth

Judging from the part he plays in Book One, *Sir James Chettam* might have been intended as a leading character in the novel, but with Dorothea's show of interest in Casaubon he fades into the background.

He is a fox-hunting squire, hearty and fresh-faced, with no regard for culture or learning; he feels it his duty to look after his farms and tenants, to fight shy of politics except to vote the same as other landowners, to ensure that no scandal touches his family, and to bequeath a flourishing estate to his heir.

Chettam is not uncouth in any way: rather he is noteworthy

for his courteous behaviour to all, including his inferiors, and for his lack of hard feelings. He has been born and educated as a country gentleman. This at times leads him to arrogance and an assumption that people must follow his advice. He is strong in his views on Brooke's political career, the need to get rid of Ladislaw, and Dorothea's marriages. Nevertheless, his advice is not taken on any of these matters, and still everything turns out right in the end. Celia admires him for his manly, authoritative way, and he loves Celia because she admires him.

The Chettam type appears in several of George Eliot's novels, and one cannot but think it is an idealized version of one of the Newdigate family whom she knew as a child and always held in respect.

His only social equal in the neighbourhood is *Brooke*. He is presented almost entirely in his own words and his character does not change one jot. Brooke has a butterfly mind which flutters from topic to topic and forgets as quickly as it shows interest. Like Casaubon, he has amassed a large collection of miscellaneous knowledge but lacks the ability and the energy to make any use of it. In every way he is thoroughly lazy. Mr Brooke has always had wealth at his disposal, he has travelled over Europe, he has read whatever he had a mind to read, and he has met numerous famous and influential men. Yet he has achieved nothing and is content to vegetate at Lowick with only the vaguest recollections of his vast experience.

Brooke is a creature of impulse and undefined whims; even his rather feeble benevolence is affected by laziness, for he can rarely be bothered to do anything about his good intentions. Thus he is a tolerant uncle and a bad landlord; he lets everyone have his own way because opposition or even clear-thinking causes him too much trouble. He wants to see both sides to a question, to urge moderation in everything, to take time before coming to a decision, all because he is afraid to take sides and too comfortable to stir himself.

One feels no sympathy when he makes a fool of himself on Nomination Day. Nor do the other characters have any sympathy for him: they put up with his rambling conversation, his involved platitudes and his genial insistence on never budging for anyone.

The agent to both these landowners is *Caleb Garth*, partly based on George Eliot's own beloved father.

At first he is depicted as rather naïve, a bankrupt who is still far too ready to trust people. He may have no head for business as it is known in Middlemarch, but he is a first-class estate manager and, like Lydgate, has a streak of idealism and imagination which causes him to feel the exhilaration of living at the beginning of a new era, in his case the age of machinery.

Garth knows that he has been a sore trial to his wife because of his unbusinesslike ways, but his honesty and unaffected love have gained for him a devoted family. He is a husband quietly admired by his wife and a father loved by his children. He is the genuine philanthropist, for he has no money to spare and still seeks to do good. When troubles appear, he can bear them because he is at ease with his own conscience; his only suffering is the knowledge that the people he loves will be forced to suffer with him.

As an estate manager he is respected by all: thus he obtains his reward. Not only does he gain more of the work he delights in doing, no matter how fatiguing, but he is able to train Fred Vincy in a career to the young man's liking, and is instrumental in bringing about his own daughter's happiness.

The Garth story may sound sentimental, but as he is the character nearest to being thoroughly praiseworthy, the reader may believe that he deserves to end his days in happiness without any detraction.

Some minor characters

The servants of the large houses play next to no part in the novel. However, it is worth noting that *Mrs Abel*, the housekeeper, brings about the death of Raffles and so hastens the downfall of Bulstrode, and a maid is instrumental in causing a great misunderstanding between Dorothea and Ladislaw, for she allows the former to see the latter in a compromising situation with Rosamond.

Of the lowly inhabitants of Middlemarch there is very little, too. Apart from the election mob (Chapter 51) there is only *Mrs Dollop*, the garrulous and scandal-mongering land-lady of the Tankard public house in Slaughter Lane (Chapters 45, 71). She is the chief propagator of anti-Lydgate gossip and, as one might expect, she is loud and long in her claims that she always knew Bulstrode to be a hypocrite. She pours out her 'information' and comments while all in the bar speak only to agree – Dill the barber, Limp the shoemaker and Crabbe the glazier.

Outside in the fields are slower, old-fashioned people, not given to much talk. Of course *Dagley* has a great deal to say about his miserable lot, but he is drunk (Chapter 39) and unexpectedly finds himself in a position to tell his landlord what he thinks of him. *Hiram Ford*, the waggoner (Chapter 56), can see no further than his fear of losing business be-cause of the railways; his prejudiced, dull mind is easily stirred to hatred of the 'Londoners', and equally quickly he is calmed into accepting whatever the future has in store for him. *Timothy Cooper*, being older and having suffered longer, knows that there is nothing that will help the poor farmhand. His fate is to endure and hope that nothing worse will ensue.

One has little contact with the wives of well-to-do townsmen. To see *Mrs Plymdale*, *Mrs Hackbutt*, *Mrs Sprague*, etc. following their normal leisure habits one has to turn to Chapter 74; and the chief value of the tea-party is to act, along with the group of men at the Green Dragon, Mrs Dollop's group and the townsmen at the meeting to deal with the new burial ground, as illustrations of the ill-will which besets Bulstrode.

The men of Middlemarch are close-knit, except for *Mawmsey* the grocer, who is of a lower social rank. He is seen (Chapter 45) 'jocosely complimentary, and with a certain considerate abstinence from letting out the full force of his mind', interested only in keeping his customers. However, he manages to remain uncommitted in politics after Brooke has visited him, and he – like his betters – has no regard for Lydgate.

Among the citizens who matter are *Standish* the lawyer (Chapter 10) 'who had been so long concerned with the landed gentry that he had become landed himself' and has picked up the tricks of their speech; *Chichely* the coroner, very much against anyone like Lydgate who threatens his position (Chapter 16), but always ready to be charming to the ladies, for he is very conscious of his own distinguished appearance; *Powderell* the retired ironmonger with evangelical leanings; *Hackbutt* the rich tanner who is given to lengthy and fluent speeches; and *Bambridge* the horse-dealer (Chapter 23) who is ' "given to indulgence" – chiefly swearing, drinking, and beating his wife', and is responsible for bringing Raffles's story to public knowledge (Chapter 71).

Borthrop Trumbull the auctioneer is a loud-mouthed, apparently cheerful man with 'nothing more than a sincere sense of his own importance' (Chapter 32). At Featherstone's home he is the one hearty figure, making himself pleasant to Mary Garth in a heavy way, and deriving much satisfaction from the secrets which he suggests are in his safe-keeping. As both man and auctioneer he is shown most clearly in Chapter 60.

The chief enemy of Bulstrode is *Hawley* the town clerk. He never liked the banker; he is readiest to make use of the scandal; and it is he who launches the final attack on Bulstrode when the latter is foolish enough to attend the meeting (Chapter 71). Hawley shows his importance by always being pressed for time; but this sense of urgency is a cover for his irritability and violent bitterness, especially when he is dealing with 'Any cursed alien blood, Jew, Corsican or Gypsy'. He is the most unattractive of a group of leading citizens who among them all can provide very few commendable aspects of character.

Equally unpleasant are Featherstone's relations. About them, too, is not the slightest suggestion of humour. Indeed, their unpleasantness is made more distasteful by their seeking after money, and even by being in need of it. Their attitude to the man who disappointed them of their pickings is well summed up by Jonah, who disgustedly says, 'I'll put a white hat and drab coat on tomorrow', as he strides away from the funeral party (Chapter 35). *Young Cranch* with the squint is half-idiot and *John Waule* hangs awkwardly about looking at Mary Garth. *Jonah Featherstone* with 'cold detective eyes' studies the situation at Stone Court, and *Brother Solomon* for all his bland manner suspects everyone of trying to get the better of him. Most important· of them is *Mrs Waule*, who despite her money, is so mean as to be concerned only with getting more. In Chapter 12 one meets her 'chill-looking purplish tint' and her face noteworthy for having 'mere chinks for eyes, and lips that hardly moved in speaking', and there, as always, she is busy making mischief for her own advantage.

As *Joshua Rigg* had apparently had to suffer considerably in the course of his life, and unexpectedly gains possession of the Featherstone estate to the chagrin of the most objectionable relations, he might have been a not unattractive character. But no. In appearance he is repulsive: 'prominent eyes, thin-lipped, downward-curved mouth, and hair sleekly brushed away from a forehead that sank suddenly above the ridge of the eyebrows'. Thus he is in Chapter 35. His habits are equally distasteful, for his 'low characteristics were all of the sober, water-drinking kind', and even when he takes a firm stand against his hated stepfather Raffles and confronts him with all the misery that he has brought on both mother and son (Chapter 41), he is 'sleek, neat, and cool as the frog he resembled'.

Raffles appears in the novel in order to present the story of Bulstrode's past and help in the delineation of Bulstrode's character. George Eliot sketches him as a melodramatic villain, a 'florid and hairy' swaggerer who has never done a day's honest work; he is a shabby sponger and at the same time a bully and a pitiless criminal. He will accept money from anyone for any reason, he has no compunction about how to raise money, and whatever money he has goes on himself alone, mostly for strong liquor. It is drink that causes his death, and drink, too, that brings about the revelation of Bulstrode's scandalous past: the banker was willing to pay for Raffles's silence, but Raffles could no longer keep a secret; his boastful tongue was always inclined to say too much, and so it divulges to all the information which has brought him a considerable amount of money (Chapters 53, 60, 61, 69).

Style

The over-all completeness of the novel is so satisfying that
one hesitates before studying the technique and style in
detail. However, there a number of important matters which
must be considered independent of each other.

Diversity of tone. The main plots are love stories; although
George Eliot is quite incapable of portraying romantic love
or violent passion, she deals with the origins and course of
love. However, in many parts of the novel there is depicted
the conflict between the claims of the intellect and of the
emotions, the value of things of the mind rather than those
of the heart. In the background are always the events of
history – the Reform Bill, new scientific discoveries and
theories, and the questioning of the long-accepted founda-
tions of society. Satire, or at least the pointed disapproval
of certain people and their acts, is yet another aspect of
the novel. Though George Eliot is not a creator of humorous
characters, she can pick out the humour of people's talk
and present flashes of conversation which are amusing in
many different ways; sometimes they are sarcastic as when
she deals with Brooke's remarks on political matters, sometimes broadly comic as in the ludicrous 'vulgarity' of the
tradesmen and their wives. Then, a considerable part of the
novel is given up to the story of Bulstrode, part tragic,
part melodramatic, a mixture of satire and social realism.
The tone of the story is forever altering, though to no
noticeable pattern, So, the reader moves from precise narrative to carefully selected bouts of conversation, from background information to comments on events of the moment,
from rapidly sketched descriptions to elaborate construction
of a situation through the mouths of a number of characters.

Diversity of tempo. To maintain the reader's interest, especially in so long a story as this, the speed at which a novel progresses must be varied; the form this variation takes will be affected by the variety of tone. At times George Eliot suspends the development of one plot so as to move on to another which will speed or slow the course of the novel as a whole; the introduction of minor or less interesting characters may take away some of the sense of urgency; comments and speculations can be profound or witty enough to make one give attention to them rather than to the narrative in which they are embodied; a stretch of dialogue may seem to make the novel progress much faster, and yet at times it can take up considerable space without moving the plot much further forward. The leisurely opening of the novel about the Brookes at home in Book One can be contrasted with the speed of events which involve Bulstrode in Book Seven.

To vary the tempo and to maintain strict relevance, there is need at times for *economy of presentation*, e.g. the compressed story of Bulstrode's first marriage. Despite the great length of the novel, the author is rarely prolix. She carefully collected background information in her notebook 'quarry', as she called it, and neatly wove it into the narrative, so that it never obtained unnecessary prominence. Despite the difficulties arising from serialization, she found means to prevent the bare recapitulation of past events to jog one's memory, and the stimulation of interest by means of action unimportant to the main plot. Not only are the various plots interwoven without loose ends, and characters made important in more than one plot, but George Eliot frequently uses a single incident to move forward more than one plot. As he is a doctor, Lydgate visits a number of characters and is able to participate in a number of different plots; the death of Raffles involves not just Bulstrode and Lydgate but, to varying degrees, Rosamond, Mrs Bulstrode, Ladislaw, Fred Vincy, Dorothea and quite a few minor characters. As every action springs from previous actions, one cannot ignore events which occurred before the time of the novel; sometimes brief narrative, sometimes casual hints that grow into plain statements, sometimes references scattered over many chapters produce essential information about the past lives of Bulstrode, Ladislaw and Lydgate. The complexity of the story and the close inter-relating of events lead to a certain amount of coincidence; but coincidence is considered to be an unfair trick of the novelist only if it seems blatantly unlikely and if the working out of the plot depends on it. Neither of these weaknesses is found in *Middlemarch*.

Attitude to characterization. The main characters are considered in detail elsewhere in this book, but one is bound to realize what a vast range of people are presented in the novel from Sir James Chettam to Dagley, from Casaubon to Raffles, from Dorothea to Mrs Dollop.

George Eliot sees character, temperament, personality to be thoroughly involved with environment; they are the result of their surroundings and can never be separated. She believes that life consists chiefly of apparently unimportant acts, the full consequence of which cannot be understood at the time; so people find themselves confronted by dilemmas they never envisaged. One is made to consider what results when Dorothea desires to become a learned woman, when Bulstrode decides not to reveal the whereabouts of a widow's child, when Lydgate flirts with Rosamond. George Eliot studies and analyses motives, describes the resulting act, and then follows it through to its consequences, taking care to treat everything in detail and to ensure that the reader sees the act as part of a series of acts. Farebrother tells Dorothea, 'character is ... something living and changing'; so each major person in the novel is forever developing, each change causing other changes, all of which are consistent with the character as originally portrayed. One is made to consider not just a certain type of woman called Dorothea, but the emotional and intellectual progress of Dorothea from a nineteen-year-old at Tipton Grange to the wife of Ladislaw, a writer and politician in London; Ladislaw himself is seen developing from a poor-relation amateur artist to a member of the Reformed Parliament. Most important, one views the rise and fall of people not only in the eyes of the world but in their own estimation and according to their own conscience.

The sense of control. The outstanding success of this novel is due to its being a unity. George Eliot presents a full picture of provincial society of the middle classes, and in doing so she clearly shows her own moral attitude. By nature she was inclined to philosophical studies, and she wrote on philosophical subjects: in *Middlemarch* she writes of people and their acts so that one may better understand how to conduct one's own life. Her point of view and the strength of her convictions are all the more effective because there is very little direct moralizing. Instead, the story infers and explains its own moral, and everything in it has been selected to serve that purpose.

On occasions one is allowed to consider an incident from several points of view so that one's own attitude is influenced by the attitude of others. Lydgate's debts, to take just one example, must be considered as he himself sees them, and as they are considered by Rosamond, Bulstrode, Vincy, the tradesmen of the town, the rival doctors and Dorothea. Even so apparently a private matter as Dorothea's second marriage must be seen from the standpoint of Chettam, Celia, Brooke and the dead Casaubon.

To exert over-all control, George Eliot has to stand outside the events, skilfully manipulating the comings and goings of

her characters; at times, however, she introduces explanation
and comment, sometimes through the mouths of her dramatis
personae and sometimes as an external spectator who feels
impelled to intrude for a moment. Readers may feel that
this intrusion destroys the illusion that the events of the novel
are real happenings. But authors of the nineteenth century
were quite satisfied to do this; and one may believe that it
emphasizes the feeling that everything in the novel has been
selected for a purpose by someone deeply concerned with
human motives. When in Chapter 15 she writes, 'I have to
make the new settler Lydgate better known to any one interested', one may consider that she is rather like a showman
putting forward a new exhibit; more skilful is her intrusion in
Chapter 40 where she acts rather like a television camera
tracking in from a distance, 'The group I am moving towards
is ...' and in Chapter 42 where she joins the reader, so to
speak, in giving an opinion of a character as if it had been
created by another author, 'Instead of wondering at this
result of misery in Mr Casaubon, I think it quite ordinary ...'

Carefully and almost unobtrusively the reader is guided by
George Eliot through the complexity of her greatest novel
and is left with the sense of having witnessed a single unified
episode in human existence. Henry James, one of the great
novelists at the turn of this century, appreciatively wrote,
'Each [plot] is a tale of matrimonial infelicity, but the conditions in each one are so different and the circumstances so
broadly opposed that the mind passes from one to the other
with that supreme sense of the vastness and variety of human
life, under aspects apparently similar, which it belongs only
to the greatest novels to produce.'

The language of the novel. So thorough is her analysis of acts
and motives that George Eliot has been forced to use a very
great number of words. But so logically constructed are even
her longest sentences, so carefully described her line of reason-

ing, that one finds little difficulty in reading *Middlemarch*: when difficulty is encountered it is caused by the profound nature of the thought or the subtlety of analysis and not by the means used to express them.

However, George Eliot assumes that the reader has a considerable background knowledge of literature both English and foreign, music, art, history, mythology, science, theology, etc, and therefore, without affectation or even explanation, makes numerous allusions to those subjects. In addition, she expects one to have at least a smattering of French, German and Latin.

She has outstanding skill in seeing a person's character revealed by his face, especially his eyes, and in a few pointed sentences can sketch out not only a portrait but a characterization. This gift is best revealed in her treatment of minor personages. She has the ability, too, to catch a turn of phrase and a tone of voice, though *Middlemarch* does not present as many opportunities for exhibiting this skill as do those novels, e.g. *The Mill on the Floss* and *Silas Marner*, which deal more thoroughly with people which the inhabitants of Middlemarch would term 'inferior' or 'vulgar'.

As previously mentioned, George Eliot was not a creator of *humorous* characters; her characters here are serious or self-important, malicious or stupid, complacent or frustrated. She is, however, satirical: she sees people's weaknesses and depicts them in a lifelike manner and yet in such a way as to focus the reader's attention on them and urge him to pass some sort of moral judgement. Obvious examples of satirical characterization are Brooke and Featherstone's relatives, but certain aspects of the major figures, e.g. Lydgate, Rosamond, even Dorothea, are considered in a satirical way.

Closely linked with this attitude is the ironical turn of phrase used sometimes in a single sentence, sometimes in a whole paragraph. This form of expression also helps to show George Eliot's attitude towards people or ideas, and guides the reader towards accepting that attitude. So numerous are examples of her ironical language that only a few minor instances need be quoted. 'A useful member [of the hospital board] was perhaps to be defined as one who would originate nothing, and always vote with Mr Bulstrode' she writes in Chapter 45; the doctors are suspicious of Lydgate because he 'had not been to either of the English universities and enjoyed the absence of anatomical and bedside studies there, but came with libellous pretension to experience in Edinburgh and Paris, where observation might be abundant indeed, but hardly sound' (Chapter 18); the inhabitants of Frick 'were not ill-fed, and were less given to fanaticism than to a strong muscular suspicion; less inclined to believe that they were peculiarly cared for by heaven, than to regard heaven itself as rather disposed to take them in – a disposition observable in the weather' (Chapter 56); 'Captain Lydgate's stupidity was delicately scented, carried itself with "style", and was closely related to Sir Godwin' (Chapter 58).

It can be seen from these examples that George Eliot writes with wit, especially when she wishes to be sardonic; and that wit is sometimes expressed with an economy of words which turns her statement into an epigram. Whether she generalizes or deals with some particular point, she can be precise; and if, as she often does, she extends the original statement or judgement and elaborates it into something lengthy, she still has such firm control that each separate, exactly worded part fits into and serves to strengthen the exactly conceived whole structure, even if it runs to a lengthy paragraph.

Textual notes, chapter summaries and revision questions

Prelude

The religious idealism of St Theresa resulted in her searching for the means of giving it a purposeful application, but women of later times who experienced a similar urge have achieved little because they lacked the support of a steadfast 'social faith and order'. When there is a woman of outstanding ability, she must strive alone and eventually fail.

Book One Miss Brooke

Chapter 1

Dorothea Brooke, a beautiful girl of nineteen, lives with her uncle at Tipton Grange, near the Midland town of Middlemarch. The period is the 1830s. She is deeply religious and 'enamoured of intensity and greatness'; thus she yearns for intellectual pleasures instead of the trivialities of her class and sex. Her sister Celia is also an attractive girl, but is quite satisfied with the leisured life of the wealthy middle class. Mr Brooke, their guardian, strives to seem important and knowledgeable about everything but is obviously empty-headed and ready to leave responsibility to others.

The family is to have dinner guests – Sir James Chettam, a local landowner, and the Rev Edward Casaubon, Rector of Lowick. Dorothea cannot believe that men find her interesting; she is convinced that Celia is the object of attraction, especially Sir James's. During the afternoon, the girls examine their mother's jewels, but Dorothea refuses to accept her share for they symbolize the vanity of this world. However, she eventually takes an emerald ring and bracelet.

Pascal's *Pensées* This was a defence of Christianity against
free-thinkers, by Blaise Pascal (1623–62).

Jeremy Taylor A famous Anglican clergyman (1613–67) whose
Holy Living and *Holy Dying* were read for generations.

Mr Peel's ... Catholic Question See Political Background,
p.15.

judicious Hooker Bishop Hooker (1554–1600) was famous for
Of the Laws of Ecclesiastical Polity. He was persuaded into an
unfortunate marriage and so had to give up a promising career at
Oxford University.

pier-glass A large wall mirror.

spiritual emblems in the Revelation of St John Jewels are
used as symbols in Chapter 21 of that book of the Bible.

Chapter 2

At the dinner party Dorothea is embarrassed by the foolish
conversation of her uncle. She is interested in Sir James's
proposed improvements to his estate, but is overcome by
admiration for Casaubon, a sallow and dried-up middle-
aged scholar. She is eager to help him organize the vast
collection of notes he has made for a book on mythology.
Sir James offers her a horse so that she may hunt, and
makes veiled references to marriage, but Dorothea brushes
him aside almost rudely, and he walks off to make himself
agreeable to Celia. Dorothea has not the slightest objection
to this for she is sure that Celia is more interesting to him;
besides, she wants to devote every minute to Casaubon's
words.

Locke John Locke the philosopher (1632–1704).

you may as well ... hounds Improving your estate is as
expensive as keeping a pack of hounds for fox-hunting.

Adam Smith *The Wealth of Nations*, by Adam Smith (1723–90).

Southey's *Peninsular War* *The History of the Peninsular War*,
by Robert Southey, was published over the period 1823–32.

the Waldenses A religious sect in France, persecuted as heretics in the seventeenth century.

Wilberforce ... philanthropy William Wilberforce (1759–1883), the famous Whig politician, philanthropist and pillar of the Evangelical church, led the campaign for the abolition of the slave trade.

cochon de lait Sucking-pig.

animals with a toilette Nothing but brute beasts which are dressed well and made to look attractive.

Mawworm of bachelors Mawworm is a sanctimonious hypocrite in Bickerstaffe's play *The Hypocrite* (1769).

Chapter 3

Casaubon confides to Dorothea his theories on the development of mythology; she in turn tells him of her belief in the 'submergence of self in communion with Divine perfection'. She is overawed by his apparent wisdom; he confesses to the need for youthful companionship and rouses in her hopes of marriage. The next day, Dorothea imagines herself guided by this wonderful scholar to a complete understanding of her environment and the knowledge which is its heritage.

Her daydreams are interrupted by Sir James, bringing her a puppy. She refuses it, but suggests that Celia would appreciate such a present. However, she immediately agrees to assist Sir James in his scheme to build cottages according to the plans she had devised for her uncle's tenants, but which Mr Brooke has scorned. Celia realizes that Dorothea may consider marrying Chettam just so as to re-plan and improve his estate.

The two men again visit the Grange, Sir James to discuss the model cottages, Casaubon to talk about mutual philosophical interests in such a frank, lucid way – or so it seems to Dorothea – as to appeal to a young girl's understanding.

She has an uneasy feeling, however, that she is guilty of pride in her own cleverness.

the earlier vintage of Hippocratic books The collection of Greek medical works (Corpus Hippocraticum) contains few genuinely old books which may date from Hippocrates himself (460–357 BC), the most celebrated physician of antiquity.

Bossuet Jacques Bénigne Bossuet (1627–1704), the greatest of French preachers in the seventeenth century.

Augustine Saint Augustine, who was both scholar (doctor) and man of God. (The Church father, 354–430, not the first Archbishop of Canterbury.)

Rhamnus A small coastal town close to Athens where there are the remains of two temples.

custos rotulorum Keeper of the local records. This is hardly a task for Mr Brooke, who cannot keep his own personal records in any organized manner.

Fijian The people of Fiji in the Pacific. George Eliot is satirizing the current taste for 'tall barricades of frizzed curls and bows'. Her own hair was always plain.

Chloe ... Strephon ... Miss Pippin ... young Pumpkin Symbols of young people in love, the former in Classical literature, the latter in popular reading.

Female Scripture Characters A well-known book by Mrs F. E. King (1813).

Sara The wife of Abraham, and **Dorcas**, raised from the dead by St Peter (Acts 9, 36–42), feature in the Old and New Testaments respectively.

Pascal See note p.**00**.

Loudon's book *A Manual of Cottage Gardening, Husbandry and Architecture* (1830), by J. C. Loudon.

Lazarus at the gate The beggar dependent on a rich man's charity. (See Luke 16, 20–25.)

spirit of Oberlin J. F. Oberlin (1770–1826), a French Protestant reformer and philanthropist.

Chapter 4

In a conversation between the two sisters, Celia says that, according to common rumour, Sir James will marry Dorothea. The latter feels revulsion for the suggestion. However, she is rather downcast when Casaubon dismisses her cottage plans as 'fads'. Mr Brooke later tells Dorothea that Casaubon had called to ask permission to propose marriage. Her uncle is obviously against the match and praises the qualities of Sir James Chettam: he sees the clergyman as an infirm, middle-aged, melancholy man without any useful ideas. Dorothea is, of course, delighted at the news.

nullifidian A sceptic.

discouraging presence One of the many creatures which tried to destroy Christian's faith, as described in Bunyan's *Pilgrim's Progress* (1678).

poor Romilly Sir Samuel Romilly (1757–1818) favoured law reform, Catholic Emancipation and the abolition of slavery. He committed suicide three days after his wife's death.

If Peel stays in See Political Background, p.15.

Chapter 5

Dorothea reads Casaubon's letter proposing marriage: it is without reference to love, but he offers her a share in a life 'unsuited ... to the common order of minds'. Mr Brooke still hopes that she will eventually prefer Chettam, but does not oppose her acceptance of Casaubon. When Celia is told, she is shocked and so averse to the marriage that her sister is quite annoyed. When Mr Casaubon visits the Grange, his lack of warm affection is never noticed by Dorothea. The ceremony will take place in six weeks' time, and they will live in his neighbouring mansion, for the rectory is considered fit only for the curate.

sonnets to Delia A collection of pleasant but shallow sonnets by Samuel Daniel (1592).

Chapter 6

As Casaubon leaves, there arrives Mrs Cadwallader, wife of the local rector. She comes of an aristocratic family, though married to a poor clergyman, and her opinion is of great importance. She accuses Mr Brooke of having political aspirations and of supporting the detested Whigs even to the extent of being willing to marry Dorothea to one. He admits that he would have liked to see her married to Chettam, but seizes the opportunity of Celia's arrival in the room to run off without telling Mrs Cadwallader the startling news. Celia informs her, and they agree that the projected marriage with Casaubon is a mistake; however, Celia believes that Sir James would be an unsuitable husband for her sister.

Mrs Cadwallader goes off immediately to Freshitt Hall and meets Sir James. He is dismayed by the news. Then the rector's wife passes on Celia's opinion, and urges him to marry the younger girl. Whatever Sir James's views, he goes immediately to the Grange.

Thirty-nine Articles The essential beliefs of the Church of England, in the Anglican *Book of Common Prayer*.

varium et mutabile semper Contrary and always changing your mind.

poor Stoddart This may be a reference to Sir John Stoddart (1773–1856).

the Moravian Brethren The Moravian Church of Bohemia was famed for its missionary work and enthusiasm for education.

A great bladder ... rattle in The bauble of the jester was made out of a bladder containing peas; thus the fool made a lot of noise by means of 'emptiness'.

Seven Sages The wise men of ancient Greece.

Sappho's apple In one of her poems, Sappho, the best-known poetess of ancient times, compares a young bride to an unplucked apple.

Chapter 7

Dorothea wishes to prepare herself to be useful to a scholar, and is eager to make a start on Latin, Greek and even Hebrew; besides, she looks on knowledge, the basis of truth, as a masculine privilege which she yearns to share. Casaubon begins to teach her, with no great enthusiasm, and she is not a clever pupil; his dislike of music suggests that he does not respond to what is artistic or emotional. By this time, Mr Brooke has come to accept the thought of the forthcoming marriage, and envisages Casaubon as a future bishop.

Milton's daughters When John Milton, the poet, became blind, he was dependent on his daughters to read those books he needed for his studies.

Gluck, Mozart Gluck (1714–87) and Mozart (1756–91) wrote operas that were produced in Vienna.

the great organ at Freiberg Aloys Mooser (1770–1829), the famous organ builder, constructed this instrument at Freiberg in Switzerland.

Henry of Navarre Born and bred a Protestant, he eventually became King Henry IV of France.

Chapter 8

Sir James Chettam still visits the Grange, and Dorothea is now far more tolerant of him, though he himself is convinced that the marriage is a mistake. One day he calls on Mr Cadwallader, and begs him to use his influence to dissuade Dorothea, or rather to convince Mr Brooke that he should make her wait until she comes of age. However, Cadwallader refuses to interfere: he knows that Mr Brooke has no strength of will, and, moreover, he thinks that Casaubon has some good qualities. A reference to Casaubon's aunt who married a Pole and thereby estranged her family – which left its money to Casaubon instead – prepares the reader for a later development in the story.

perversity of a Desdemona Desdemona, the young and
  beautiful daughter of a Venetian nobleman, insisted on
  marrying Othello, a coloured man, much older than herself.
Xisuthrus Xisuthrus was the Babylonian Noah; 'Fee-fo-fum' is a
  sneering reference to Jack and the Beanstalk. The tone of the
  remark is contemptuous. cf. the reference to 'Hop o' my Thumb'
  later.

Chapter 9

Mr Brooke, Dorothea and Celia drive over to see Casaubon's
house; it has 'an air of autumnal decline' and nothing much
will be done to brighten or modernize it. Dorothea's boudoir
will be in the room, now much faded, used by Casaubon's
mother. However, she seems quite satisfied with arrangements. A disappointment is that the nearby village is in no
need of assistance or philanthropic gestures by anyone.

  In the garden she meets a gentleman with a sketch-book;
it is Will Ladislaw, the grandson of Mr Casaubon's unfortunate aunt. After attending public school he had gone to
Heidelberg University – a strange choice for a gentleman
of those days – but now has no plans for a career except that
he wants to travel. He obtains a poor opinion of Dorothea
because of her conversation and her readiness to marry so
dull a man as Casaubon, but her voice greatly attracts him,
and he is eager to maintain their acquaintance. Casaubon
obviously considers the young man to be a foolish wastrel.

Renaissance-Correggiosities Antonio da Correggio
  (1494–1534) painted many Madonna and Child pictures;
  evidently, religious art of this type did not appeal to Dorothea –
  or to George Eliot.
brio Liveliness.
morbidezza The subtle, almost imperceptible, gradation of
  tones in painting.
Aeolian harp An instrument hung where the wind could blow
  on its strings, thus producing a very soft melodious sound.

Bruce or a Mungo Park James Bruce (1730–94) explored
Abyssinia and the Blue Nile; Mungo Park (1771–1806) mapped
the course of the River Niger.

geognosis Knowledge of the earth's surface.

a Byron, a Chatterton, a Churchill Mr Brooke reveals his lack
of taste and his old-fashioned views as his names form an anti-
climax. Lord Byron the great Romantic poet was still very
popular in George Eliot's day; Thomas Chatterton (1725–70)
wrote pseudo-romantic verse; Charles Churchill (1731–64) was a
satirist in the conventional classical manner.

Chapter 10

Six days later Casaubon informs Dorothea that Ladislaw has
left for the Continent with the vaguest of plans for the
future. The bridegroom-to-be is quite unmoved by the
thought of the forthcoming marriage; he sees his wife merely
as an admiring audience to encourage him in his studies.
Dorothea looks forward to her marriage as a 'higher
initiation in ideas'. The honeymoon tour will extend as far
as Rome, where Casaubon will work in the libraries; he
cannot understand why Celia will not accompany them, for
she would provide company for his wife, who otherwise is
bound to feel lonely. For the first time Dorothea is annoyed
with him; he had said, 'I should feel more at liberty' if
Celia was with them.

Mr Brooke gives a last dinner-party before the marriage,
and a number of people important to the later story are
introduced – Mr Vincy the new Mayor, Mr Bulstrode the
banker, and others. During the conversation, Mrs Cadwallader prophesies that within a year Dorothea will hate
her husband. The guests then discuss the new doctor, Tertius
Lydgate, a man of good family and one who has impressed
Lady Chettam. He is philanthropically inclined and has
decided views on new ideas in medicine and public health.

De Quincey's Thomas De Quincey (1785–1859) the famous essayist, was an addict of opium and wrote *Confessions of an English Opium Eater.*

an immortal physicist Presumably Thomas Young (1773–1829), the physicist and Egyptologist.

Stoics and Alexandrians Stoicism expounded by Zeno emphasized the importance of factual knowledge and the control of emotion. Neo-Platonism, which was originally connected with Alexandria, was a philosophy of mysticism and idealism at the expense of factual knowledge.

Broussais François Broussais (1772–1832), a famous surgeon and physician.

Franciscan tints Possibly his paleness is compared with that of St Francis the ascetic; on the other hand, the phrase may refer to the colouring of paintings by Pietro della Francesca.

Chapter 11

The Vincys are well-established manufacturers. Rosamond Vincy, who has refused the attentions of the best local young men, attracts Dr Lydgate. Her brother Frederic is a dashing fellow who has failed his examinations at university and is now content to do nothing except live well. He has gained a poor opinion of Lydgate from their previous conversation.

Fred Vincy is likely to be left a large sum of money by his uncle Featherstone and therefore visits the old man's home, Stone Court, whereas Rosamond detests going there. The petulant invalid is nursed by Mary Garth, who is related to him by his first wife (Fred is a nephew by the second marriage); she is a most pleasant woman but poor. One sees that she attracts Fred, almost as much as the hopes of Featherstone's money.

the solar guinea The gold coin which was the basis of the monetary system. It was not minted after 1813.

at John's At St John's College, Oxford.

Ar hyd y nos The Welsh air 'All Through the Night'.

Chapter 12

Next morning, when Rosamond and Fred ride over to Stone Court, they meet Mrs Waule who is also visiting; she is Featherstone's sister and wishes to keep the money in the family rather than have it bequeathed to one who, she says, is notorious for his loose living. She also mentions that the Vincy business is declining. Mr Featherstone has no illusions about anyone.

In a clumsily humorous fashion he accuses Fred of borrowing money on the security of his future inheritance (for so Mrs Waule has spitefully told him). This is not true, though Fred has boasted of his expectations. Featherstone then insists that his nephew should obtain from Bulstrode a letter stating he no longer believes that Fred has been trying to raise money this way.

In the meantime Rosamond is fishing for information from Mary about Tertius Lydgate, who is due to pay his usual call on his patient. Thus one understands Rosamond's sudden interest in Stone Court. Rosamond tells Mary that Fred has refused to become a clergyman; Mary agrees with his decision for she is certain he would be a most unsatisfactory one. She also assures Rosamond there is no need to fear that Fred may marry her, for should he propose, she will refuse him. However, she is quite put out when Lydgate calls and pays great attention to Rosamond, who makes no secret of her interest in him. One remembers that she had always intended to find romance with someone who was not a native to Middlemarch.

Fred is very worried about approaching Bulstrode, for his request will worsen still more the relations between the banker and Mr Vincy. Ironically, Mr Featherstone had invented the tale about Bulstrode. To add to his troubles, Rosamond informs him that Mary has no interest in him.

an articled pupil Apprentice teacher. Instead of paying fees at school she would assist with the teaching.

Josephus, Culpepper ... *Magazine* Flavius Josephus (AD 37–100) wrote *The Jewish War*; Sir Thomas Culpepper was a seventeenth-century writer on usury; Friedrich Gottlieb Klopstock (1724–1802) wrote a religious epic, *Messias*; *The Gentleman's Magazine* (founded in 1731) was a sedate, conservative periodical.

il y en a pour tous les goûts There is something for all tastes (every man to his taste).

old Overreach Sir Giles Overreach was a cruel usurer whose villainy is the theme of *A New Way to Pay Old Debts* (1633), a comedy by Philip Massinger.

Revision questions on Book One, Chapters 1–12

1 Show how the following pairs of characters are studies in contrast: Dorothea and Celia; Rosamond and Mary; Casaubon and Sir James Chettam.

2 By what means does George Eliot show that both Casaubon and Mr Brooke are foolish men, and that Ladislaw and Fred Vincy are wastrels?

3 Contrast the views on marriage held by Dorothea, Sir James and Casaubon.

4 What impressions of Anglican clergymen do you obtain from this section of the novel? You should refer to Casaubon, Cadwallader and Tucker.

5 Make careful notes on contemporary events and subjects of national controversy mentioned by George Eliot.

6 What picture is painted of the lives of the upper-middle-classes in and around Middlemarch?

Book Two Old and Young

Chapter 13

Bulstrode is meeting Lydgate in order to discuss the organization of the new fever hospital built and equipped at the former's expense. He realizes that the appointment of Lydgate as superintendent will not be popular with the local doctors but he recognizes the newcomer's zeal; besides, he wants someone to support him in his insistence that religion will play an essential part in the routine of the hospital and that the Rev Tyke will be appointed chaplain rather than the local vicar, Farebrother, whose views clash with Bulstrode's Evangelicalism.

One of the committee which assembles is Vincy and he, having been told by his son Fred of the embarrassing demand of old Featherstone, gives a rather inaccurate account of the incident to Bulstrode and asks him to clear Fred of the slanders. Although they are brothers-in-law, Vincy and Bulstrode have little regard for each other. The latter makes religion and moral issues somehow the reasons for his refusing to help Fred, and the most he will do is consider the matter at his leisure.

Chapter 14

Apparently influenced by his wife, Bulstrode relents and next day sends the required letter. Featherstone rather grudgingly accepts it and then gives Fred a present, the disappointingly small sum of £100.

Fred stays on at the house to see Mary Garth. There is more disappointment, for she reproaches him with his lack of a profession and even admits that she rather despises him. He urges her to marry him and so bring about an improvement in his nature but she refuses: he will never alter except perhaps by means of hard work.

When he reaches home, Fred gives his mother £80 to keep safe for him: the truth is that he owes £160 and his debt has been backed by Mary's father who is in no position to pay it.

Brenda Troil ... Mordaunt Merton ... Minna ...
Cleveland All these are characters in *The Pirate* (1822), by Sir Walter Scott.

Waverley ... Flora MacIvor Characters in *Waverley* (1814), by Sir Walter Scott.

Olivia and Sophia Primrose The Vicar's two daughters in *The Vicar of Wakefield* (1766), by Oliver Goldsmith.

Corinne The heroine in the novel of that name (1807) by Mme de Staël.

a bill An IOU in the days before cheques were used. If there was doubt about the credit of the person giving the bill, he would be expected to have it signed by a reputable person, who would thus accept responsibility for paying the money when demanded.

Chapter 15

The history of Lydgate is recounted. An orphan accustomed to genteel poverty, he had been apprenticed to an apothecary; he had worked assiduously to become a doctor because he visualized such a career as an 'alliance between intellectual conquest and social good'. Because he was eager to reform the practice of medicine, he had left London and its corrupt ways; moreover, he wished to pursue research into the structure of tissues. At the time under consideration, he is still suffering from the shock of an experience in France.

He had become infatuated with an actress. One night she killed her actor-husband on the stage, and there was some doubt as to whether the death was accidental. Their friendship became even more intimate, but then she suddenly left him and only after much trouble did he track her down at Avignon. Then she told him that she had meant to kill her husband.

A great historian A reference to the novelist Henry Fielding (1707–54) and his *Tom Jones* (1749).

Rasselas *Rasselas, Prince of Abissinia* (1759), by Samuel Johnson.

Gulliver *Gulliver's Travels* (1726), by Jonathan Swift.

Bailey's Dictionary The forerunner of Dr Johnson's.

Chrysal A satirical novel (1760–65), by Charles Johnstone.

'makdom and her fairnesse' Companionship and beauty, here used rather slightingly as merely conventional terms.

old Troubadour strings A reference to the love songs of the Middle Ages sung by Minstrels: George Eliot considers them to be lacking in any sincerity.

London, Edinburgh, and Paris His residence at those places implies that he had the best possible medical education. Scottish universities were then famous for their training of doctors, and Paris University was a great centre for research.

Jenner Edward Jenner (1749–1823) is particularly famous for his discovery of vaccination.

graduates of Oxford and Cambridge The passage is heavily sarcastic. The medical training at both universities was notoriously inadequate; there was next to no control over people who pretended to be doctors or who were incompetent despite their having obtained a degree in medicine.

Herschel Sir William Herschel (1738–1822), the famous astronomer, discovered Uranus, then believed to be the farthest of the planets.

a recent legal decision The Apothecaries Act of 1815 insisted on qualifications for what we call dispensing chemists. Lydgate acts on the assumption that a doctor can leave dispensing to a chemist, whereas his colleagues expect to profit from making up their own medicines.

Bichat François Bichat (1771–1802), one of the pioneers in the study of the nature of disease. This type of work necessitated much post-mortem examination and in France there was far less prejudice against the dissection of dead bodies than in England.

cultus Acquired tastes.

pew-renters Well-to-do members of the congregation who pay
an annual sum to reserve a special pew in church.

the Saint-Simonians People sympathetic towards the views of
the Comte de Saint-Simon (1760–1825), a socialist of sorts and a
champion of the rights of women.

Offenbach's music George Eliot evidently considered that the
operettas of Jacques Offenbach (1819–80) were trivial and
indicative of lack of good taste in music.

Porte Saint Martin The best known of the melodrama
theatres, and, to English people, a rather 'shady' place.

a Provencale She came from Provence in the deep south of
France, and therefore, to the English sense of logic, was very
passionate.

Chapter 16

Conversation at Vincy's dinner party shows that Bulstrode's
administration of the hospital is not popular but that his
power in the town is indisputable. Lydgate's important
remarks about medical reforms are also unacceptable.

The young doctor is attracted by the charm and accomplishments of Rosamond Vincy; however, he admits to himself that he is in no position to marry and that his interest in
medical research makes life pleasant enough. Rosamond considers him to be superior to the local young men because
he is distantly related to an upper-class family, and therefore assiduously cultivates her attractions. Her aunt, Mrs
Bulstrode, understands Rosamond's chief weaknesses –
frivolity and extravagance.

Mr Farebrother, the local vicar, also visits the party, and
his comparative poverty is revealed; worse, he plays whist
for money to eke out his salary.

black draught A cheap laxative prescibed without much
thought for its value to the patient.

Wakley Thomas Wakley (1765–1862), doctor and founder of the world-famous medical periodical *The Lancet*, made constant demands for reforms in his profession. One of his contentions was that coroners should be men with medical rather than legal qualifications.

prick-eared Priggish.

plucked Fred Fred who has failed his examinations.

He has an ear He can appreciate good music.

Kapellmeister The person in charge of music at the court of some German nobleman. Although such a post required much work and was usually ill-paid, many a famous musician depended on it for an assured income.

Black-eyed Susan . . . Batti, batti A very strange mixture. 'Black-eyed Susan' was a song from a popular English ballad-opera of no musical value; Haydn's canzonets are short songs, artificial in form and sentiment; *Voi, che sapete* and *Batti, batti*, though rather sentimental, are very moving arias from *The Marriage of Figaro* and *Don Giovanni* respectively, both operas by Mozart. One suspects that Rosamond sang them all alike, and badly.

like a Niobe before her troubles Niobe with her seven sons and seven daughters had shown some contempt for Leto with only twins. But these were the gods Apollo and Artemis, who destroyed every one of the children.

Louis Pierre Louis (1787–1872) was a French physician who conducted valuable research on typhoid fever.

Lalla Rookh A highly romantic poem (1817) by Thomas Moore.

Chapter 17

We are introduced to the shabby genteel home of Mr Farebrother, Vicar of St Botolph's, and his women relations. Although he could well do with a £40 p.a. salary as chaplain to the hospital, he is quite tolerant of Mr Tyke, who, Bulstrode insists, should have the post.

They are visited by Lydgate, whom Farebrother knows by

repute because he used to correspond with the man sharing the former's rooms in Paris. While discussing the inhabitants of Middlemarch, the Vicar warns the young doctor not to thwart Bulstrode, who can easily become a bad enemy. Another name that is mentioned is Mary Garth's, but Farebrother seems unwilling to talk about her.

anencephalous Lacking in brains.

Aphis Brassicae A garden pest feeding on cabbages.

Philomicron Lover of the trivial. By inventing such a pen-name the Vicar shows his contempt for would-be scholars. The *Twaddler's Magazine* also suggests that such people write a good deal about nothing of importance.

a sort of Pythagorean community A utopia for those who practise socialism. It was possibly inspired by his reading of Saint-Simon (see note p.98). Ironically, Lydgate's own career ended much the same as Trawley's.

a German bath A spa in Germany.

Robert Brown A famous botanist (1773–1858). The work referred to appeared in 1828.

Chapter 18

Lydgate is attracted to Farebrother as a man, but is greatly concerned that a clergyman should be so ready to find dubious means of obtaining money to supplement his stipend. The doctor, being a member of the hospital committee, must vote for either Tyke or Farebrother. His dilemma is accentuated because he does not enjoy being patronized by Bulstrode and yet he wants the post of hospital superintendent. If he votes against Tyke – Bulstrode's nominee – he will antagonize the man who controls his career at Middlemarch.

On the committee there are a number of Bulstrode's opponents, and the local doctors are set against any innovation. When Lydgate arrives, the committee has voted on the appointment and the result is a tie: Lydgate's vote will decide the matter. He supports Tyke, thus making himself appear to be Bulstrode's underling.

Prodicus ... the Nessus shirt A Greek writer who told of how Hercules, in his youth, met two beautiful women, Pleasure and Duty, and had to take his choice; he preferred the latter. Nessus, the Centaur, when dying from the poisonous arrows of Hercules, had told the hero's wife that a shirt steeped in his blood would revive her husband's love if it ever waned. Later, she sent him the shirt, and he died horribly.

Chapter 19

The scene changes to Rome. Ladislaw and his friend Naumann are studying works of art in the Vatican when the latter is struck by the beauty of a young lady. This is Dorothea Casaubon. Naumann wants to paint her portrait and urges Ladislaw, as a relation of her husband, to seek permission. He refuses. His friend threatens to paint her without his aid, and accuses him of being jealous.

the most brilliant English critic William Hazlitt (1778–1830).

long-haired German artists Rome attracted many artists from Germany and some twenty years before the time of the novel there was a group of these, with a religious leaning, called the Nazarenes.

Belvedere Torso A greatly admired statue of the first century AD, the subject of which cannot be identified.

Geistlicher The clergyman.

Schön, schön All right, all right.

Antigone She was the daughter of Oedipus, and the Greek ideal of devotion to a parent. Thus Naumann considers Casaubon as Dorothea's father rather than her husband.

genialisch Original or ingenious.

Plastik Sculpture.

Der Neffe ... ungeheuer! The nephew is more important than the uncle.

Chapter 20

In her sumptuous apartment, Dorothea is crying, for she realizes that she is 'a mere victim of feeling' who faces a 'new real future' with an old, dull, dry bookworm whose search after knowledge has produced and can produce nothing of value. Although the Casaubons are on their honeymoon, Dorothea is neglected by her husband; he prefers to study manuscripts.

For the first time they have actually quarrelled; she had suggested that Casaubon should end his preparations and start writing his book, but this is what he is obviously afraid to do. Annoyed with each other, they visit the Vatican, and there Ladislaw sees them.

judicious Hooker See note p.84.

Farnesina A gallery in the Vatican Palace.

Raphael Raffaello Sanzio (1483–1520), then the most admired of Italian painters. Casaubon is dutifully conducting her round the sights of Rome.

Cabeiri Fertility gods. George Eliot infers that they were so obscure and unimportant that only a man like Casaubon would be interested in them.

Chapter 21

When Dorothea is sitting unhappily in her apartment, Ladislaw calls. She is delighted and they are soon talking about art, showing considerable interest in each other's views. However, he does not intend to be an artist; indeed, he lacks the will to follow any career.

Ladislaw shows his dislike for Casaubon, and shocks Dorothea by explaining that her husband's work is not only unoriginal but is based on long out-of-date opinions. He wonders why she ever married such a man.

Mr Casaubon returns and the contrast between the two

men is most obvious. Because of her recent experiences and Ladislaw's statements, Dorothea is moved by the 'first stirrings of a pitying tenderness fed by the realities of his lot': Casaubon cannot respond to her devotion but he is in need, she thinks, of someone to sustain him through his dull and disillusioned life. Therefore, she apologizes for her behaviour earlier that day. Casaubon is apparently jealous of the young man, though he is polite in a cold way.

a Bat of erudition In his search after obscure knowledge, Casaubon is like a bat – dry, blind to the world around him, living only in the dark.
Ariel The happy spirit with magical powers in *The Tempest*, by Shakespeare.
If Mr Casaubon read German The best contemporary scholarship in religion and philosophy was being written by Germans; Casaubon is, therefore, completely out of touch with modern ideas and his work is valueless from the start.
he had ... centre of self He too had a personality which needed to be developed by contact with others. Dorothea imagined that only she could profit from their relationship.

Chapter 22

At dinner the next evening, Ladislaw is such a pleasant conversationalist that both Casaubon and his wife talk freely. He even convinces the former that he should take Dorothea round a few of the artists' studios before he leaves Rome.

They visit Naumann's studio, obviously carefully prepared in advance, and that painter makes a great impression on them. He flatters Casaubon into sitting for a sketch of himself as Thomas Aquinas, to be incorporated into a larger work; having contrived that a number of sittings will be required, he suggests filling in the time by painting Dorothea as Saint Clara. Ladislaw's views of this are mixed – he is delighted to enjoy more of her company but dislikes

Naumann's familiarity with her. Casaubon buys his own portrait, but not his wife's.

Thus Naumann has achieved his desire to paint the beautiful woman seen in the Vatican, but Ladislaw is infuriated; he had taken her to the studio to satisfy his own vanity in showing off this attractive relation and not to have his friend captivated by her charm.

So strong are his emotions that Ladislaw calls on Dorothea when he knows they will be alone in the house, and they discuss their interests in art and poetry. He protests against so young a woman fated to miss the enjoyment of life by being bound to an old man in a dull house. However, Dorothea accepts this state, and is even annoyed when Ladislaw again tells her that Casaubon's work is valueless; indeed, she warns him never again to criticize her husband's writings. However, she soon forgets her irritation because of Ladislaw's genuinely warm regard for her, and they express the hope of meeting again soon, for he is returning to England where he will live without being dependent on any one.

When Casaubon returns, Dorothea tells him of Ladislaw's praiseworthy resolve, but her news obtains a chilly reception.

Middleton Conyers Middleton (1683–1750), whose work on theology was by then thoroughly outdated.

the Madonna ... the Laocoon A Madonna painted by Raphael. It was commissioned by Sigismondo Conti in gratitude for his escaping death at the siege of Foligno. The Laocoon is a Greek statuary group carved about 50 BC and restored in the 16th century according to the advice of Michelangelo. George Eliot apparently considers these to be the finest examples of their kind.

Thorwaldsen A Danish sculptor (1770–1840) who lived in Rome.

Marlowe's Tamburlaine A painting illustrating a scene from *Tamburlaine the Great*, a play by Christopher Marlowe (1564–93).

pfuscherei Rather a mess.

His walk ... *belles-lettres* i.e. his is a writer's career.

Minotaurs Mythical creatures whose food is beautiful women, a reference to the monster kept in Crete and destroyed by the hero Theseus.

Paracelsus He lived from 1493 to 1541 and achieved outstanding fame in chemistry, surgery, alchemy and magic.

Bryant Jacob Bryant (1715–1804) had covered much the same ground as Casaubon was trying to do, and was already discredited and out of date.

Chus and Mizraim They were said to be grandsons of Noah and the ancestors of the ancient Egyptians.

porte cochère A porch which provides shelter for a coachman awaiting his master.

Revision questions on Book Two, Chapters 13–22

1 Describe the appearance and interests of Casaubon and Ladislaw so as to show the great contrast between them.

2 What do you find praiseworthy about Lydgate as a doctor, and as a man?

3 Explain how Book One and Book Two of this novel are effectively linked by means of the plot and the characters.

4 What do you consider to be Dorothea's attitude towards Casaubon by the time they reach the end of their honeymoon?

5 To what extent is it true to state that Fred Vincy is a decent young man who merely lacks a sense of responsibility?

6 What is there to suggest that Rosamond Vincy is not likely to prove a satisfactory wife to Lydgate?

Book Three Waiting for Death

Chapter 23

The reader must cast his mind back to the events of Chapter 14, for the present episode deals with Fred Vincy, who is so certain of his ability to judge a horse's worth that he owes Bambridge the horse-dealer a considerable sum. Worse, payment of the debt has been guaranteed by his friend Caleb Garth.

Yet Bambridge is due to be paid; Fred has not the money and dares not ask his father for it; Garth will not be able to pay for he is a bankrupt who is assiduously working to repay every penny of his own debts. Fred had therefore given £80 out of Featherstone's £100 into his mother's safekeeping. He intends to use the balance as stakes in gambling. He quickly loses it.

Then he decides to sell his own horse at Houndsley Fair, and takes the £80 with him. With Bambridge and Horrock the vet, he goes off to a stable in the midst of the slums to view a supposedly valuable horse; in the end he is the victim of smart practice by the 'horsey' men, and gives his own mount plus £30 for a hunter which he hopes to re-sell at a profit.

'duck under' Economize.

Lindley Murray and Mangnall's *Questions* Two very widely used school text books were *English Grammar* (1795), by Lindley Murray, and *Historical and Miscellaneous Questions* (1800), by Mrs R. Mangnall.

'cute jockeys Horse-dealers who are near to being swindlers.

chyle-fed blood Healthy blood fed with fluid derived from food.

blacklegs Horse-racing swindlers.

goes on ... sawyers Its breathing is so noisy that it sounds as if twenty men were sawing wood.

Chapter 24

Three days later, Fred realizes that the recently bought horse is unsaleable; therefore he decides to confess the situation to Garth and give him the remaining £50.

When he reaches the house he finds Mrs Garth especially happy because her son Alfred is to be apprenticed as an engineer with the £92 she has saved for his premium. When Garth comes home and Fred tells him of the £160 debt which must be paid with only £50 to meet it, he displays no hard feelings; nor does his wife, who has been ignorant of this commitment. Alfred's career will have to be sacrificed for the sake of the premium money, and Mary Garth is to be asked for her savings amounting to £20. Thus Fred's debt can be paid, and he has never even asked his wealthy father for the money.

'Lindley Murray' See note p.106. Obviously George Eliot regards the book as out of date.

his prince of darkness Literally the Devil, it here refers to the sort of person whom Garth considers to be the worst possible.

Chapter 25

Fred goes to Stone Court and confesses everything to Mary Garth, who is quite outspoken in her reproaches; she even asks him to seek more money from Featherstone. Fred is full of miserable self-pity, convinced that he is nothing but the victim of misfortune and therefore deserving of other people's sympathy and charity. Mary wonders how she can love so contemptible a man.

Caleb comes to ask for her savings; he warns her that Fred will bring her nothing but worry and suffering, as he himself did to her mother, but she assures him that she will never marry anyone who lacks 'manly independence'.

Mrs Piozzi's recollections *Anecdotes of the Late Samuel Johnson*
(1786) were written by an intimate friend of his, Hester Thrale,
later Mme Piozzi.

Chapter 26

While walking through the slums of Houndsley (see Chapter
23), Fred had caught an infection which Wrench, the
family doctor, neglected. Because Lydgate is passing near
the Vincy house, he is called in; he diagnoses the illness
as typhoid fever, aggravated by wrong treatment. He suffers
considerable embarrassment when Mrs Vincy asks him to
take over the care of the patient, and Wrench disagrees
with his method of treatment, which seems sheer quackery.

The situation becomes the subject of gossip in Middlemarch, and it is even said that Lydgate is Bulstrode's
illegitimate son.

the usual white parcels The medicines dispensed at his own
surgery.
Niobe-throat i.e. smooth and rounded like that of the Greek
statue of Niobe (see note p.99).

Chapter 27

Because Lydgate is attending Fred Vincy, he and Rosamond
see a good deal of each other; he thoroughly enjoys the
prolonged flirtation – for that is all he means it to be – but
Rosamond is discreetly preparing the way for their marriage.
The young men who flock round Vincy's daughter whenever
they can are most disgruntled with Lydgate; for his part, he
finds far more interest in medical research and the feud with
the local doctors about the conduct of the hospital.

Mary Garth discourages Fred by not communicating with
him during his illness, and when Lydgate suggests that his

patient should recuperate at Stone Court, where Mary is staying, Mrs Vincy strongly objects.

Then one day a servant of Sir James Chettam summons Lydgate to Lowick Manor.

the last *Keepsake* The latest issue of *The Keepsake*, the most fashionable of expensive annual gift-books.

Lady Blessington The Countess of Blessington (1789–1849) wrote novels about aristocratic society and edited *The Keepsake*.

L. E. L. The pen-name used by Letitia Elizabeth Landon (1802–38), a writer of poems and fashionable novels.

Chapter 28

The reason for this summons is not yet given, for the reader is now reintroduced to Mr and Mrs Casaubon, who have returned to Lowick Manor.

Dorothea has given up all hope of achieving any close relationship with her husband and is already depressed by the house in which she must live. Moreover, Casaubon is quite unwell. She can understand something of the feelings of the woman who ran away from Lowick Manor and eventually became Ladislaw's grandmother.

Mr Brooke and Celia visit her and bring some cheerfulness. To Dorothea's delight, Celia announces that she is engaged to Sir James Chettam.

Chapter 29

Casaubon, too, is disillusioned; there is no sign of a child to be his heir; he has come to suspect that his great work will be treated with as little respect as had been some earlier pamphlets; and he is no longer certain of his religious faith. He is reluctant to start writing the book, partly because his wife is eager to help him and she may thereby realize his inability. He decides to publish a pamphlet first.

Ladislaw writes to Casaubon suggesting he should visit the Manor, and he encloses another letter for Dorothea. When Casaubon informs his wife that he has told Ladislaw not to come, she is so angry at not being consulted that she leaves the room without reading either letter.

While Dorothea is trying to calm herself by working at her studies, the door opens and Casaubon staggers in, obviously very ill. Luckily, Celia arrives on her last visit before marriage, and with her is Sir James, who sends off his servant for Lydgate. Thus the reader is brought back to the events of Chapter 27.

Sir James is sympathetic towards Dorothea; he had once hoped to marry her and he had seen her throw herself away on Casaubon. From now he vows to be 'her brotherly friend'.

'Parerga' Works of secondary importance.

Brasenose Brasenose College of Oxford University.

the big mask and the speaking-trumpet Devices used by actors on the ancient Greek stage to give a larger-than-life dignity to their appearance and magnify their voices. Yet, says George Eliot, behind these awesome trappings were ordinary men.

Warburton Bishop William Warburton (1698–1779) engaged in numerous theological controversies.

viros nullo aevo perituros Men who will never perish. In 'the next age', both they and their little reputations will have perished utterly.

'newborn babe' Pity is so described in Shakespeare's *Macbeth*.

Chapter 30

Although Casaubon slowly recovers, Lydgate warns Dorothea that he could die quite suddenly and that he must guard against strain or anxiety. He suggests some form of relaxation, but Casaubon will have none of it.

Only now does she read Ladislaw's two letters; he has decided to return to England so as to earn a living, but without relying on any assistance from Casaubon; he intends to call at Lowick Manor with the painting bought from Naumann in Rome.

Dorothea realizes that he must not visit her, and asks her uncle, Mr Brooke, to write putting him off. Brooke, however, becomes so interested in the young man that he invites him to stay at Tipton Grange with him. He has a vague plan that Ladislaw may assist him in a political career by editing the *Middlemarch Pioneer*, which Brooke has just bought.

Smollett Tobias Smollett (1721–71) wrote novels in which satire and broad comedy were the outstanding features.

Chapter 31

Fred goes to Stone Court to convalesce, but Rosamond accompanies him lest he shows too much interest in Mary Garth.

Mrs Bulstrode and Mrs Plymdale exchange views on Lydgate's relations with Rosamond; that young lady evidently prefers the doctor to Mrs Plymdale's son. Mrs Bulstrode goes off to have a talk with Rosamond, who does not deny her feelings but admits that Lydgate has not yet proposed; the older woman stresses the reasons why Lydgate is unacceptable as a husband and urges the merits of young Plymdale, but to no avail.

Mrs Bulstrode then tells her husband to discover the doctor's intentions; from his enquiries he learns that Lydgate has none. She herself then goes off to confront him and to beg him not to obstruct the efforts of less attractive men. At first, Lydgate is so selfish and vain that he sees no reason why he should not continue his mild flirtation; nevertheless, he eventually decides to call on the Vincys only for professional reasons.

After ten days without seeing him, Rosamond grows desperate. Luckily, Mrs Vincy meets Lydgate and asks him to call when he has further news of Mr Featherstone's health. He does so, and finds Rosamond alone. His impersonal attitude causes her so much embarrassment and anguish that she is on the verge of tears, and it is then that he feels what he thinks is love for her; he kisses her and proposes marriage. Mr Vincy readily agrees, partly because he is in a very good humour, for Featherstone is likely to die soon, and then he is sure that Fred will come into a fortune.

Mademoiselle de Montmorenci He makes a flirtatious comparison with some beautiful heroine of fiction.

Orlandos Unrequited lovers. The reference is to the hero of Shakespeare's *As You Like It*.

lashed to the mast ... the sirens The beautiful Sirens were supposed to lure sailors to their doom on savage rocks; to avoid being tempted towards them, Ulysses tied himself to the mast of the ship and so was able to sail a straight course past them.

stage Ariadne The Ariadne of legend helped Theseus to kill the Minotaur (see note p.105); he swore eternal faith but soon deserted her. Rosamond sees herself as such a woman, but pictures the situation as it might appear in a contemporary sentimental play.

Forget-me-nots under the water Blue eyes bathed in tears.

where the chain went How he might be forever bound to her, and what might be the result of his being tied in marriage.

Chapter 32

As Featherstone is becoming weaker, all his relations visit him frequently and some even insist on staying the night at Stone Court, causing trouble to Mary Garth. The old man despises them all.

Borthrop Trumbull, the auctioneer, takes most notice of Mary. He is actually allowed to see the invalid and comes down from the bedroom with much show of mystery, hinting that Featherstone's money will be left to someone outside the family; he gives the impression that this someone will be Mary.

Brobdingnag specimens In this context, people who are outstandingly unpleasant. Brobdingnag was the land of giants in Swift's *Gulliver's Travels* (see note p.97).

when Borrow ... Testament An incident from *The Bible in Spain* (1841), by George Borrow.

Three Crofts and the Manganese Firms in which Featherstone held shares.

Blue-Coat land Land on which will be built some charitable institution such as a free school.

Murillo ... Vandyck As all the painters mentioned are of international fame, and therefore their works are very expensive, one must assume that Trumbull could not tell a genuine picture from a fraud or a copy.

Chapter 33

In the middle of the night, Mary is keeping watch by the dying Featherstone and worrying lest Fred will be disappointed of the legacy.

At 3 a.m. the old man wakes, quite clear-headed. He tells Mary to burn the will in the iron chest. She refuses, as such an action would be misinterpreted; he then offers her a considerable amount of money from a tin box but she remains firm in her decision. Featherstone then begs her to bring Fred Vincy to him; she insists on waiting till later in the day. So enraged is he that he throws his stick at her; a little afterwards, imperceptibly, he dies.

carrying their fools' caps unawares Having foolish ideas without realizing how foolish they are.

Revision questions on Book Three, Chapters 23–33

1 Explain the reasons for Casaubon's changed attitude to Ladislaw.

2 Show clearly how the strain between Casaubon and his wife steadily increases, taking care to explain the hidden fears which afflict the former.

3 What impression of Fred Vincy do you obtain from the account of his activities in Book Three?

4 By reference to any two minor characters in Chapter 33, illustrate the means by which George Eliot produces vivid portraits of middle-class people.

5 Give an account of how Lydgate becomes so involved with Rosamond that he eventually proposes marriage.

6 'The older ladies of Middlemarch are chiefly concerned with making or preventing marriages.' Illustrate this statement by reference to some of the incidents described in Book Three.

Book Four Three Love Problems

Chapter 34

Featherstone has the 'handsome' funeral which he himself arranged.

Casaubon resumes his studies despite all warnings, and is anxiously watched by his wife, Celia and Chettam, now her husband. Brooke arrives and announces that he has brought Ladislaw with him. Casaubon is very cold in his greeting, and assumes that Dorothea has arranged for Ladislaw to stay at Middlemarch to be near her. Ironically, Brooke hopes that the young man will help *him* with *his* notes, while Mrs Cadwallader suggests that he will write speeches to assist Brooke in his political career.

Harpagon The chief character in *The Miser*, by Molière
  (1622–73).
a lien Certain rights over the property.
tithe A 10% tax on land, payable, sometimes in kind, to the
  local clergyman.
omne tulit punctum Everybody agrees with it. This may be
  just one of the hackneyed 'right quotations'.

Chapter 35

Featherstone's relations are gathered to hear the reading of
the will; they are united only in showing their antagonism
to the Vincys. Among the visitors is Mr Rigg, a most un-
prepossessing man unknown to all except Mary, who has
met him on two previous visits to Stone Court.

  Mr Standish, the solicitor, is ignorant of the contents of
the latest will, for it had been drawn up by another firm.
He reads the earlier will first: by it, some of the relations
obtain small legacies, but Fred Vincy is to have £10,000 and
Rigg is to inherit the remainder. The second will causes
consternation to nearly everyone: Stone Court and the estate
are left to Rigg and the remainder is to be used for founding alms-houses. Later it is revealed that Rigg is Featherstone's illegitimate son.

  Fred Vincy is infuriated. With no legacy he will have to
become a clergyman in order to earn a living and he
detests the prospect of such a career. Mary Garth's suggestion
that he will be all the better for not having the inheritance
is rudely brushed aside.

Christian Carnivora The so-called Christians who were
  interested only in 'eating up' Featherstone's wealth.
batrachian Frog-like.
last bulletins ... Duke of Clarence See Political Background,
  p.15. The Duke became King William IV.
phaeton A light four-wheeled open carriage.

margrave A nobleman. Presumably one might interchange the two without noticing any difference.
loobies Country bumpkins.

Chapter 36

Mr Vincy is now not only exasperated by Fred's lack of a career but is annoyed that Rosamond is engaged to a man with little money, though he is too much a coward to broach the subject with Lydgate himself. Mrs Bulstrode urges Vincy to interfere, and even tries – though unavailingly – to persuade her husband into using his influence.

Rosamond expects to live grandly when she is married, and Lydgate assumes that he will maintain the standard of living expected of a well-to-do gentleman. He still has the illusion that marriage will provide the calm and freedom he needs for medical research.

When Rosamond tells him that her father is thinking of ending the engagement, Lydgate begs her to hasten the date of the wedding. So firmly does she demand her father's consent to their plans that he weakly agrees, on condition that Lydgate insures his life.

Now that all is settled, Rosamond insists that Lydgate should inform Sir Godwin and his important relations of the coming marriage, for she hopes to be invited to stay with them; she is determined that they must leave the vulgar society of Middlemarch and make a career elsewhere. Mrs Vincy openly says that she hopes Sir Godwin will settle a sum of money on the married pair.

Eros The Greek name for Cupid, classical god of love.
Valenciennes A very fine type of lace (from the town of that name).

Chapter 37

The *Pioneer*, owned by Mr Brooke, is putting out a great deal of propaganda in favour of his becoming a Member of Parliament, and it is rumoured that Ladislaw will be taken on as editor. However, as Brooke is a careless and mean landlord, local opinion is that he should first reform his own estate.

Casaubon is more antagonistic than ever towards Ladislaw. The latter is in love with Dorothea and dedicated to making life pleasant for her; she is still determined to give all the help she can to Casaubon but realizes that he is only the shadow of a man. When Ladislaw maintains that her husband cannot bear anyone to assist him and therefore see what he has done, because he himself is unsure of its value, she is not indignant, nor does she deny the truth of it. As their talk grows more and more intimate, he admits that Casaubon had looked after him and his mother as soon as he heard of their poverty. He asks her opinion as to whether he should stay in Middlemarch and edit the *Pioneer*. Dorothea is keen that he should but then recollects that, in view of their difficult situation, Casaubon should be consulted.

Ladislaw had called on this occasion because a shower of rain drove him to seek shelter, and he was near the Manor; it so happened that Casaubon was out. When he returns, more cheerful than usual – he has been praised for his scholarly work – he is told by Dorothea of Ladislaw's visit and the chances of his obtaining work on the paper. This news immediately kills the little warmth between the two of them that had existed for a short time. Next morning, Casaubon writes to Ladislaw insisting that acceptance of such a menial post would be 'offensive' to him.

Because of Ladislaw's information about his early life, Dorothea feels sorry that his mother and grandmother suffered at the hands of the Casaubon family. She decides to change her will so that Ladislaw will be assured of the income he deserves as some slight compensation. When she and her husband lie awake in the middle of the night, she tells him of her plans and suggests that her part of the estate should be given up to Ladislaw. Casaubon's answer is a downright refusal.

Next day, Casaubon receives a letter from Ladislaw refusing to be intimidated. He sees no means of dealing with the situation – though he never doubts Dorothea's fidelity – except by saying nothing about it to anyone and forbidding Ladislaw to visit Lowick Manor under any circumstances.

dark-blue freemen Dark blue was the colour used to signify one of the political parties. Freemen were privileged to be the only voters in some towns. Mr Hawley displays the prejudice that existed between the gentlemen of the county (where voters were landowners) and the inhabitants of towns.

Huskisson William Huskisson (1770–1830), financier and politician, was an advocate of moderating the Corn Laws and encouraging free trade.

Shelley Percy Bysshe Shelley (1792–1822) is considered here as the young romantic poet burning with zeal for political reforms. Brooke goes on to say that Ladislaw does not suffer from Shelley's objectionable immorality and atheism.

the Delectus A collection of passages in Latin or Greek for translation as a school exercise.

Dante ... Laura The love of Dante for Beatrice and of Petrarch for Laura is known the world over through the sonnets which those Italian poets wrote. George Eliot maintains that the nineteenth century is more prosaic, less ecstatic, and that lovers can express themselves in conversation better than in sonnets.

holy skulls and other emptinesses Ladislaw visualizes the dull Casaubon as nothing but dry bone on which a beautiful woman's love is being wasted. George Eliot shows her contempt for the veneration of holy relics.

Lowth Probably Robert Lowth (1710–87), the theological scholar who disagreed with some of the views put forward by Bishop Warburton (see note p.110).

Chapter 38

Mr Brooke is to be put forward as Whig candidate in the forthcoming election. Sir James Chettam is against this, and says that Ladislaw is likewise opposed; he is particularly concerned that Brooke is notorious as an irresponsible landlord, and wants him to take on Mr Garth again to manage his estate. His advice, the *Trumpet*'s attack on Brooke's bad husbandry, and Mrs Cadwallader's warning about the rough treatment to be expected at an election, all leave the would-be MP quite unaffected.

Brougham and Useful Knowledge Henry Brougham (1778–1868) was one of the most energetic of radical reformers. He was partly responsible for the founding of the Society for the Diffusion of Useful Knowledge, which greatly helped the dissemination of liberal opinion.

a Byronic hero Ladislaw had been compared with Shelley; now it is with Lord Byron (1788–1824), the heroes of whose poems are projections of himself. To Mrs Cadwallader they are glib-tongued young men devoted to conspiracy and amorous adventures.

modus Money paid in lieu of a tithe. (See note p.115.)

Lafitte Jacques Lafitte (1767–1844) was one of the leaders of the 1830 Revolution in France.

The Edinburgh *The Edinburgh Review*, founded in 1802, was one of the most authoritative critical periodicals. Its Whig politics would appeal to Brooke.

fiat justitia, ruat . . . Let justice be done even though the heavens fall. Brooke cannot remember a Latin tag which every schoolboy in those days must have known.

Chapter 39

Dorothea is able to see Ladislaw again when Sir James takes her to Stone Court; it is then that she is told for the first time that he has been forbidden to enter Lowick Manor.

They must stay parted. So changed is Dorothea that she
no longer prays, and she confesses that she has no enthusiasms
or ambitions.

Nevertheless, she tells her uncle that he must make sweeping changes on his estate and begin by repairing his cottages.
Brooke points out that Chettam, for all his fine talk, preserves game and is harsh with poachers, whereas *he* is going
to deal lightly with a lad who has just been caught killing
a rabbit.

Brooke goes to visit the boy's family, and there is a
description of the tumbledown cottage and neglected land.
Dagley, the tenant, comes back drunk from market; he shows
no respect for his landlord and instead of being grateful for
the comparatively generous treatment of his son warns
Brooke that the projected Reform Bill will put an end to
bad landlords. Details of his very bad reputation in the
district quite surprise Brooke.

emollit mores Civilizes one's nature.

Young Edward Young (1683–1765) is chiefly known for *The
Complaint, or Night Thoughts* which was standard reading for
generations.

the Far Dips were cut The corn was cut in the outlying field
called the Far Dips.

kick your own trough over Bring about the destruction of the
place that feeds you. Mrs Dagley knows that Brooke can turn
Dagley out of his tenant farm.

Chapter 40

Mary must find new work now that Featherstone is dead,
and reluctantly she decides to accept a teaching post at
York. The family fortunes, however, are suddenly saved:
Garth is asked to manage Sir James's estate and to assist
with the Brooke property.

Mr Farebrother comes on behalf of Fred who has been

away from Middlemarch for some time; he brings the young man's farewell, for he is going back to university, reluctantly accepting the career of a clergyman. As Fred is the topic of conversation, Mrs Garth tells Farebrother of Featherstone's dying request to Mary.

It is obvious that the Vicar is greatly in love with Mary, but he is too poor and has too many family commitments ever to marry.

Mr Garth unintentionally depresses Farebrother's hopes further by suggesting that, as he is now going to be a much busier man, he needs an assistant, and Fred would be an excellent choice. He also mentions that he has been asked to value land for both Rigg and Bulstrode.

costly letters This was before penny postage, and the cost was borne by the recipient of the letters.
Cincinnatus The great Roman general was recalled from disgrace because he was the only man capable of saving the city from invaders.

Chapter 41

At Stone Court, Rigg refuses to give any financial aid to John Raffles, his disreputable stepfather who has long made life miserable for both Rigg and his mother.

Before he goes, Raffles asks to have his brandy-flask re-filled; as it is loose in its case, he wedges it with a piece of paper picked up from the hearth. This is a letter from Bulstrode.

Uriel An archangel who was given control of the sun. His name means 'God is my light'.
father-in-law Stepfather.
now it had done for Huskisson Huskisson (see note p.118) was killed by one of the locomotives present at the trials of Stephenson's *Rocket* (1830).

Chapter 42

Casaubon is bitter because of the supposed injuries he has suffered; he sees Dorothea's devotion as 'a penitential expiating of unbelieving thoughts', and her care for him as an expression of superiority, criticism, even rebellion. He is intensely jealous of Ladislaw, who can control and guide Dorothea's judgement. He is determined to protect her against adventurers after his death.

He summons Lydgate to find out his expectation of life; as he is suffering from fatty degeneration of the heart, he may die suddenly or live for another fifteen years. After Lydgate's departure, Dorothea comes to cheer her husband; however, she is coldly received. She is incensed by his attitude, realizing that Casaubon wishes he had never married her, but convinced that he is to blame for the situation.

She makes up her mind not to join him at dinner, but Casaubon sends first to tell her that he will spend the evening alone in the library. Dorothea sits up late, waiting for him to finish work, and they are reconciled by her example of devotion.

sciolism A pretentious smattering of knowledge.

Laennec Paul Laennec (1781–1826) was a pioneer in studying the heart; he also invented the stethoscope.

dark river-brink This is a reference to the Greek idea of death. Dead souls congregate on the bank of the River Styx and wait for Charon, the boatman, to ferry them across.

In the jar of her whole being In the shock which her entire being felt.

watching Keeping awake.

Revision questions on Book Four, Chapters 34–42

1 Explain clearly the nature of the three love problems.

2 Show how, step by step, Casaubon grows colder towards Dorothea owing to his work, and to Ladislaw.

3 Write a description of Dagley's farm so as to illustrate the unfortunate state of many agricultural workers at the time.

4 What impression do you obtain of Rosamond after she is engaged, and later married, to Lydgate?

5 Is it fair to consider that the Garth family and the events which befell it are quite unbelievable? Give your reasons.

6 Give an impression of Lydgate and his medical work from the standpoint of a local person who disliked him.

Book Five The Dead Hand

Chapter 43

Dorothea decides to visit Lydgate in order to discover the nature of her husband's illness. He is out, but Rosamond – now his wife – is enjoying herself by accompanying the singing of a gentleman. It is Ladislaw who is with her. He offers to go to the hospital for Lydgate, but she prefers to make the journey herself; she is greatly embarrassed by the situation and realizes that she suspects the nature of Ladislaw's interest in Rosamond.

He, too, is mortified, for his only interest in Mrs Lydgate is the pleasure she obtains from music; when she questions him about his relations with Dorothea, he is ill at ease, so much so that she tells her husband on his return from hospital that Ladislaw is obviously a great admirer of Mrs Casaubon.

Lydgate's far more important news is that Dorothea will probably give £200 p.a. to the hospital.

Imogene The heroine of Shakespeare's *Cymbeline*.
Cato's daughter i.e. Portia in Shakespeare's *Julius Caesar*. Both characters would appear wearing Roman dress in George Eliot's day.

Diana A goddess (a Roman goddess, worshipped in various guises, but her attributes are not important here).

leather and prunella The leather apron of the cobbler is something far different from the prunella of which a parson's gown is made. Ladislaw cares nothing for social distinctions.

later than Racine Jean Racine (1639–99) was one of France's greatest dramatists. Rosamond had no knowledge of the many contemporary Romantic writers then held in high esteem.

Chapter 44

When Dorothea consults Lydgate, he tells her next to nothing about Casaubon's illness, but takes the opportunity to talk about the needs of the Middlemarch poor. Bulstrode has done much for the hospital, but there are many townspeople antagonistic to him who will therefore give no aid, and the local doctors are entirely against it. She then offers £200 p.a. of her own money.

When she tells Casaubon of her resolve, he offers no objection. However, he is convinced she knows what Lydgate has told him about the illness, and his coldness towards her is further aggravated.

Chapter 45

The antagonism towards Lydgate is found in all classes of people: some of the objections are that he is eager to conduct post-mortems, that he does not dispense drugs or even advocate medicine, and that he is so ungentlemanly as to slander his fellow doctors. Yet he has undoubtedly made some extraordinary cures, and he is still invited out because he comes of a good family. This antagonism tells against the new hospital, for none of the other doctors will support it, and Bulstrode cannot continue as its sole patron, for he needs money to buy an estate.

Farebrother dislikes Bulstrode but admires Lydgate; he warns the doctor not to become involved with the banker, and not to get into debt, for the Vicar well knows how that can hamper a man. Unfortunately, Lydgate is already badly in debt; he is living more expensively than his declining practice warrants. For all that, he is quite a happy man, because he feels that he is working at the beginning of a new era in medicine and has Rosamond to share his joy; she, however, regrets that he is nothing better than a doctor.

Burke and Hare Beginning with robbing graves, they ended by murdering people to obtain corpses for dissection by doctors. They were tried in 1828.

'squitchineal' Perhaps a mixture of squills as a laxative and cochineal as colouring matter.

'soopling' Making supple or soft.

vis medicatrix The power of medicine.

Mr St John Long A notorious quack doctor who was tried for manslaughter in 1830.

Raspail François Raspail (1794–1878) was not only a naturalist but a politician zealous for reform.

Vesalius Andreas Vesalius (1514–64), one of the great pioneers of anatomy. He roused considerable antagonism because of his dissection of human bodies.

experto crede Be advised by one who knows.

Galen A celebrated Roman physician of the second century AD. He wrote numerous text-books and greatly influenced medieval medicine.

take a great chair at Padua Become an important professor at the university of Padua, then famous for its medical studies.

Chapter 46

Brooke continues to plan his political career with the assistance of Ladislaw and the *Pioneer*; he does not want to commit himself to sweeping reforms, but Ladislaw insists there can be no half measures. The latter even visualizes the possibility of himself entering politics, assisted by Brooke.

Ladislaw is viewed with suspicion in Middlemarch: he is a 'foreigner' and far too glib a speaker, and some of his habits are eccentric. However, he is popular with children, and has a devoted band of ragged urchins whom he takes out into the countryside.

Rosamond grows very fond of him because he is so unlike her husband in his interests. Ladislaw tells Lydgate his opinions of Reform and claims that Brooke could be a satisfactory MP, especially as he has recently set about improving his estate; but Lydgate annoys him by inferring that such an opinion has been influenced by the need to keep on good terms with his patron. Ladislaw points out that much the same can be said of Lydgate and Bulstrode. The real causes of the doctor's irritable manner are that he has received a final demand for payment of a furniture bill and that Rosamond is pregnant.

Lord John Russell's measure See Political Background, p.15.
Wilberforce's and Romilly's line See notes pp.85 and 87.
political unions See Political Background, p.15.
nominees of the landed class Candidates voted into
  Parliament by landowners in order to further their own interests.
Burke Edmund Burke (1729–97), one of the greatest of the
  Whigs, achieved fame as an orator in Parliament and as a writer
  on political subjects.
I can't help ... to give you So muddled is Brooke's thinking
  that at the moment when he is concerned with the abolition of
  small, corrupt constituencies, he is wishing he could have
  Ladislaw elected to Parliament by such a place.
energumen A fanatical devotee to a cause.
galligaskins Breeches.
Stanley Lord Stanley (1799–1869), later Earl of Derby and
  Prime Minister.

Chapter 47

Owing to what Lydgate has said, Ladislaw is worried about his association with Brooke and his interest in Dorothea; to him she seems all the more delightful because he cannot hope to marry her. Despite the difficulties caused by his residence in Middlemarch, he decides to stay on since she had urged him to do so.

So upset is he that he decides to ignore Casaubon's instructions; he will see and speak to Dorothea by meeting her in church on Sunday morning. However, he feels dreadfully embarrassed during the service, and leaves without speaking to her. Dorothea is near to tears.

old Drayton Michael Drayton (1563–1631), the poet.

Chapter 48

Dorothea's distress had been caused by her husband's ignoring Ladislaw in church, since she had hoped for a reconciliation if they should meet. That day Casaubon has a relapse.

She is desperately in need of companionship, but Ladislaw must become increasingly remote from her. When thoroughly depressed, she is invited by Casaubon to help him in the organization of his notes so that she may come to understand his work; even in the middle of the night they work together. It is then he asks her to promise to carry out his wishes after his death. Dorothea refuses because she fears these wishes will be concerned with his work, in the value of which she has no faith. She can pity and help whilst he is alive, but she will not commit herself to unexplained obligations.

Next morning, Casaubon feels worse, but insists on taking a walk in the garden. Dorothea now realizes that she is bound to agree to her husband's request, and goes off to find him. He is unconscious in the summer house. When he is brought to his room, she hysterically agrees to do whatever he is planning for her, but he dies without hearing her.

Herodotus A famous Greek historian (484–24 BC).
Keble's *Christian Year* John Keble (1792–1866) published
this volume of sacred poetry in 1827.
Lavoisier Antoine Lavoisier (1743–94), sometimes called the
father of modern chemistry.
Gog and Magog Mythical beings referred to in Genesis, Ezekiel
and Revelation; they found their way into medieval legends.

Chapter 49

The gloom on the day of Casaubon's funeral is increased
by the terms of his will which infer that Ladislaw will seek
to marry Dorothea. Sir James insists that scandal can be
avoided only if Ladislaw leaves the country – is perhaps
bribed to do so – and Dorothea stays with her sister. Brooke
objects to exiling Ladislaw, for such an act might seem to
support Casaubon's suspicions.

Thoth and Dagon The first is an Egyptian god, and the second
a Philistine.
Norfolk Island At that time a penal settlement in the Western
Pacific.

Chapter 50

Dorothea is staying at Freshitt Hall but is eager to take
over the conduct of her own estate, especially the appointment of a new Rector. Celia tries to prepare her for the
news about the will, in which is the stipulation that if she
ever marries Ladislaw she must lose all the Casaubon
property. Her sympathy for Ladislaw is thereby increased
and yet she cannot now let him have the share as she had
planned. She feels revulsion against her dead husband and
his studies, instructions about which have been left for her at

home; she decides she is under no obligation to complete Casaubon's work.

Lydgate, as medical adviser, suggests that, to obtain some relief from the repression she has suffered, Dorothea should be encouraged to manage her own affairs. To her he pleads the merits of Farebrother as Rector, and, by mentioning the clergyman's weaknesses, arouses in her a desire to save him from them.

pinfold Restriction.

St Paul's Cross Because of its central position in old London, it was often used as a place for delivering speeches and sermons.

Latimer Archbishop Latimer (1485–1555) is particularly famous for the simple, vernacular style of his sermons, with many vivid and easily understood examples.

Daphnis A legendary Sicilian shepherd who is a symbol of simple, innocent and courteous love.

Chapter 51

Ladislaw knows nothing of the will, but makes no attempt to see Dorothea; indeed, he might even have left the district had it not been for the need to assist Brooke at the forth-coming election.

No matter how carefully he is prepared, Brooke cannot be trusted not to make a fool of himself. Before he addresses the crowd on Nomination Day, he befuddles himself with two sherries, and then, having forgotten even the opening of the speech prepared for him, rambles on, unaware of the ridiculous figure he is making. His opponents hoist an effigy of him, echo his words with comic results, and pelt him.

Ladislaw is so disgusted that he considers leaving Middle-march forthwith, and perhaps returning when he has received some sort of political fame; yet he decides to stay on so as to make contact with Dorothea.

Brooke is plainly told by his party that he must withdraw; the *Pioneer* will be taken over and Ladislaw dismissed. When he is informed of this, Ladislaw accepts the situation but does not change his mind about staying in the town.

Parliamentary Candidate Society Presumably this was similar to the political unions.

plumpers People who use two votes for one candidate at an election.

Burke with a leaven of Shelley See notes pp.126 and 118.

a set of couplets from Pope Alexander Pope (1688–1744) is famous for the high degree of technical skill he used when writing verse in couplet form.

the new police Sir Robert Peel had organized the first police force in 1829.

Chatham ... Pitt The Earl of Chatham (1708–78) and his son William Pitt (1759–1806) were both great Whig Prime Ministers.

'eating his dinners' Studying law. A student's attendance at the Inns of Court and at some colleges is reckoned by the number of occasions when he has dined in hall.

Althorpe Viscount Althorpe (1782–1845) was largely responsible for steering the Reform Bill through Parliament.

Chapter 52

Farebrother is to be the new Rector and will therefore have enough money to consider marriage. However, Fred returns from the university, having obtained a degree, and is reluctantly prepared to begin his career as a clergyman; he tells Farebrother of his love for Mary Garth and asks his friend to explain the situation to her and discover her feelings.

The Rector goes off to Mary: she will not promise to marry Fred, and will certainly reject him if he is hypocrite enough to enter the Church. He must achieve something in life before he proposes marriage, and she is sure that he should set his mind on some 'good worldly business'. When Farebrother asks Mary if she intends to wait for Fred to make a success of himself, his manner of speaking causes her to realize he is asking about his own chances; she feels it necessary to tell him that she is so grateful for Fred's devotion that she will never marry anyone else. To her sorrow, she senses how much she has hurt a man she greatly admires.

laches Shameful qualities.
the Articles See note p.86.

Chapter 53

Rigg wants only to set up a money-changing business; therefore he sells Stone Court to Bulstrode for his retirement. One evening, the latter has just met Garth to discuss the management of the estate when along the lane comes Raffles. To him, Bulstrode is 'Nick', whom he had known thirty years before and who had been connected with some shady business. Raffles has been trying to get in touch with him ever since he found it was his letter which had been used as packing for the brandy-flask (Chapter 41). Bulstrode is very ill at ease; he tells Raffles to stay the night at Stone Court, and they will confer early the next morning.

When they resume their conversation, Raffles speaks of a widow whom Bulstrode had married. Raffles himself had been sent to America and paid to stay there; he now refuses to go back, and he has no intention of working when money can be easily obtained. Evidently Bulstrode had planned to marry the wealthy widow but she had insisted on first trying to trace her daughter and grandchild: Raffles had found them but never disclosed his information, therefore she had married Bulstrode and left him her considerable fortune.

Raffles demands £200 without guaranteeing that he will

not return; Bulstrode offers £100 there and then, the rest soon. To make the banker even more uneasy, Raffles mentions that he discovered the name of the man who married the widow's daughter, but he cannot remember it. Shortly after Bulstrode leaves, Raffles recalls the name – Ladislaw. He writes it down, but has no intention as yet of revealing the knowledge. Then he leaves Stone Court.

'read himself' Went through the ceremony of assenting to the Thirty-nine Articles.

Warren Hastings Warren Hastings (1732–1818) was the first Governor-General of India; he was put on trial for corruption, and, though exonerated, undoubtedly made a fortune during his term of office.

bashaw Person of great wealth and social importance.

in the Dissenting line Belonging to a nonconformist church, which was then considered socially inferior to the Church of England.

Revision questions on Book Five, Chapters 43–53

1 Explain in some detail the various influences on Ladislaw which made his stay in Middlemarch uncertain.

2 What do you learn from Chapter 46 of electioneering in the 1830s?

3 For what reasons might you feel sympathy for Casaubon as he is portrayed in Book Five?

4 Explain Farebrother's state of mind towards Mary Garth, and towards Fred Vincy.

5 Do you consider that George Eliot has made plausible those parts of Book Five which deal with Bulstrode and Raffles? Give your reasons.

6 Write a character-sketch of Bulstrode at the height of his self-esteem and worldly success.

Book Six The Widow and the Wife

Chapter 54

Dorothea's return to Lowick Manor is not regarded with favour by her closest friends; she should not live alone, though not all would agree with Mrs Cadwallader that she should marry a nobleman. Dorothea is determined not to continue her husband's work; her chief desire is to see Ladislaw, but he does not call.

When at last he visits her it is to say he is leaving to study law, and may not see her for some years; after a long pause, she approves of the plan, but does not tell him of the conditions laid down in her husband's will because she assumes he knows of them.

Both are greatly moved by the situation and yet each seem capable of saying only the wrong words. To cap all, Sir James enters and his coldness makes Ladislaw all the more determined to stay away from Dorothea.

Bouddha i.e. the child treated as if it were a god. Aunt Dorothea's attitude to the baby is naturally less prejudiced than Celia's.

eat my dinners See note p.130.

Chapter 55

As a substitute for the love of Ladislaw, Dorothea takes a sentimental interest in the miniature of his grandmother. Others may talk of remarrying – though Sir James thinks it is a revolting suggestion – but she is determined not to. To give herself some interest, she plans to establish a utopian 'little colony' of workers.

Dido or Zenobia Dido Queen of Carthage and Zenobia Queen of Palmyra were women who wielded great political power. Both resisted most strenuously the attempts of men to wrest the power from them.

Chapter 56

The railway is to pass near Middlemarch, and surveyors are to be seen in the fields. They are very unpopular with the farmhands, and one of them is attacked. Caleb Garth, while busy on some work for Dorothea, assists the surveyor; then Fred who is riding by joins the fray. Afterwards he assists Garth in his work and displays an interest in learning more about it; he admits he does not want to be a clergyman, and that he loves Mary.

Garth returns home and tells his wife of his resolve to train Fred in estate management; she is far from enthusiastic, partly because she wishes Mary would marry Farebrother and people might misinterpret his interest in the young man. Fred's father, though disappointed, accepts the situation; his mother is chiefly worried about his becoming further involved with Mary.

However, when he starts work with Garth he is disgruntled to find that it necessitates a considerable amount of paper work at which he is quite incompetent, despite his university education.

There is talk of Lydgate who is ruining his practice and getting into debt, and of Rosamond's miscarriage.

hundred Sub-division of the county.

overseer of the roads Each small local authority, even a parish, was responsible for the upkeep of roads within its jurisdiction.

the war ... King George Thus briefly is given the history of a lifetime: the wars against France from 1792 to 1815; possibly the peace treaties which ended the struggle against Napoleon; the nationwide construction of canals which to him would seem more wonderful than the infant railways; old George III; and his son who, having ruled as Regent during his father's madness, eventually became George IV.

clemmin' Starving.

Age of Reason The Revolutionary period through which he had lived, when Reason was supposed to triumph over worn-out theories of despotic government.

Rights of Man The social and political privileges due to everyone, as demanded by revolutionary thinkers. Both terms are associated with the French Revolution but they became subjects of controversy in England from the late eighteenth century onwards.

Chapter 57

When Fred finds Mrs Garth at home, he realizes that she is far from pleased; when she tells him that he ought not to have sent Farebrother as an intermediary to Mary, it dawns on him that he has placed his friend in an unhappy position. Yet when he asks Mrs Garth point-blank if he is obstructing a romance, he gets no straight answer.

Fred goes to see Mary who is now assisting the Farebrother family in their removal, and the Rector makes an opportunity to leave them alone for a while. Feeling very sorry for himself, Fred assures her that no matter how well he does in his new career she will marry Farebrother; this she indignantly denies and even disclaims any deep interest in the clergyman. This latter statement worries her for she does not wish to slight a man whom she greatly respects. She refuses to go any further in stating her attitude towards Fred.

regenerate Porson Richard Porson (1759–1808) had a vast reputation as a Greek scholar. His weakness was an obsession for drink.

making a meal of a nightingale Eating the choicest food, i.e. having the best things in life.

Chapter 58

This refers back to the end of Chapter 56. On the honey-moon visit to Sir Godwin's home, Rosamond had aroused the interest of Captain Lydgate, her husband's cousin. Later he stayed with them at Middlemarch and openly carried on the flirtation. He even persuaded her to go riding against Lydgate's orders, for she was pregnant. The result was a fall and a consequent miscarriage.

By this time Lydgate has no illusions about his wife: she disregards all his wishes and advice and is still convinced that she is always right. The practice deteriorates and his debts increase; they must economize, but Rosamond continues in her accustomed extravagance.

He borrows money with his furniture as security, and also arranges to return to the jeweller some of the silver plate and the amethysts which were his bridal present. But how can he tell Rosamond of these intentions?

Lydgate reaches home in a turmoil of worries and is annoyed to find a visitor – Ladislaw, who is still living in Middlemarch. When later he tells his wife of their financial position, she puts on a show of cold duty befitting a martyr. His attempts to show affection meet with no response.

She wants to borrow from her father, to put off the inventory of the furniture, to leave Middlemarch rather than stay on humiliated. He refuses all her suggestions, and so increases her detestation. However, he will spare her jewels if she will consent to give up the silver; she continues with her air of self-sacrifice and insists on bringing him the amethysts; he refuses to take them, but is not forgiven. When Lydgate commands her to stay in the house to aid the men taking an inventory, she frigidly acquiesces.

Mechanics' Institute A centre for the education of working-men after work. A great number of such institutions received enthusiastic support during the nineteenth century.

Chapter 59

Fred rarely sees his sister as they have nothing in common
but when he notices Ladislaw leaving the house he calls to
tell her of the stipulation in Casaubon's will, news of which
is leaking out; he wishes to prevent it reaching Ladislaw's
ears.

When she tells Lydgate this choice piece of gossip, he too
begs her to keep quiet, as he himself has. Yet next day
when Ladislaw again calls on her she informs him. He is both
angry and troubled; he swears he will never marry.

chiffonnière Low cupboard with a sideboard top.

Chapter 60

Bulstrode now owns the *Pioneer*, for which Ladislaw still
works, although the fear of gossip about Dorothea and
himself provides further reason for his leaving Middlemarch.
He is asked by his employer to attend the auction of a
bankrupt's furniture in order to bid for a picture desired by
Mrs Bulstrode.

Bambridge comes to the sale, accompanied by a man he
has just met by accident, John Raffles. The latter is
obviously startled to see Ladislaw, and in the refreshment
marquee asks him if his mother had been a Sarah Dunkirk.

That evening Raffles overtakes Ladislaw in the street and
claims to have met his father in Boulogne; his mother, it
seems, had gone on the stage after running away from her
family who were high-class receivers of stolen goods. Ladislaw
is appalled to think how Dorothea and Sir James will
receive this information.

flesh-painting Large groups of nude figures. George Eliot is
  sarcastic about English people's attitude to the nude at that
  time.

Gibbons Grinling Gibbons (1648–1721) was famed for his
elaborate wood carving.

Guido Probably Guido Reni (1575–1642), the religious painter.
The low price offered suggests that the painting was a copy or
had been wrongly attributed to Reni.

Rugby men Ladislaw had been educated at Rugby school.

'Berghems' Nicolas Berghem (1620–83) was a Dutch landscape
painter.

practical rebus The symbolic representation of a word or idea
by means of an object which can be used.

a young Slender A very foolish young man. The reference is to
a character in *The Merry Wives of Windsor*, by Shakespeare.

political parasitic insects Reporters in search of political
news. Ladislaw of the *Pioneer* is a gentleman who, like many of
his contemporaries, adopted this highly contemptuous attitude
to the Press.

Chapter 61

When Bulstrode returns from a business trip he is told that
Raffles had called; there is another visit the following day,
after which Bulstrode becomes ill. He realizes that, as his
wife knows only that he gained a fortune from marrying a
widow, she will be overwhelmed when the truth is disclosed.

The truth is that, as a clever but poor bank clerk famed
locally for his religious zeal, he had become the confidential
accountant of Mr Dunkirk, a pawnbroker who was the
most influential man in the congregation. Soon he discovered
that the business was only a cover for receiving stolen goods,
but for the sake of the comfortable life he was then leading he had managed to square dishonesty with his religious
principles. The pawnbroker's daughter had run away from
home; the son died, and then Mr Dunkirk himself. The
rest of the story was as Raffles had recounted it in Chapter
53; Bulstrode had kept quiet about the daughter's whereabouts because he was sure she would waste her mother's

money, whereas he would put it to philanthropic uses. When Dunkirk's widow, now Bulstrode's wife, died, he used her fortune to set himself up as a banker, and very gradually withdrew from criminal activities.

To ease his conscience, Bulstrode makes an appointment with Ladislaw; he admits he had married Ladislaw's grandmother and had been enriched thereby, and asks to make amends for taking what should have gone to his mother. But he does not admit to having found her whereabouts years before, not until Ladislaw asks him point-blank. He offers £500 p.a. and eventually a legacy. Ladislaw's questioning is inexorable; he wants to know if Bulstrode knew that the money had been obtained dishonestly. This is more than Bulstrode will admit: there are limits to his abasement and apology.

Ladislaw will not dirty himself by accepting the money, nor could he ever explain it to Dorothea. He leaves Bulstrode weeping partly with relief, partly in humiliation.

putrefying nidus A place of corruption in which something is born.

Chapter 62

This new information makes it essential that Ladislaw should quit Middlemarch, but first he will see Dorothea. However, when he calls, she is away for the day.

Sir James suspects the purpose of Ladislaw's continued stay in Middlemarch and asks Mrs Cadwallader to mention to his sister-in-law the unpleasant gossip about Ladislaw's connection with her and Rosamond. When Dorothea is told, she indignantly refuses to think ill of him, although she cannot but feel uneasy.

On returning home, she finds Ladislaw there, collecting his sketches. He tells her he must leave, and again insists that he had never had any thought of obtaining her money. They both stand hurt and embarrassed; he is certain she must understand his real feelings; she thinks, for a moment, that he is speaking of love for her but dismisses the thought, believing he refers to Rosamond.

His parting words reveal to Dorothea his true meaning, and she is left alone overcome with joy. She calls her carriage and sets off to overtake him; but when she reaches the walking figure, she passes without a word. She sees him as a man who cannot imagine her defying her husband's will, and he sees her as a rich woman unconcerned for a poor man.

'weepers' The black veil worn by a widow in those days.

Revision questions on Book Six, Chapters 54–62

1 Trace the course of Dorothea's relationship with Ladislaw, emphasizing the misunderstandings and embarrassments which both suffered.

2 What are your views on the value of Farebrother's self-sacrifice in giving up all thoughts of marrying Mary?

3 Briefly describe three incidents which illustrate the tension and disillusion which now mark the lives of Lydgate and Rosamond.

4 Explain Dorothea's attitude towards Casaubon's wishes after his death.

5 Give a concise account of Bulstrode's career before he married his second wife.

6 Describe the state of affairs between Bulstrode and Ladislaw after the latter had learnt of Mrs Dunkirk and her daughter.

Book Seven Two Temptations

Chapter 63

Although Lydgate is making a success of the hospital his practice is still declining and his debts are increasing.

At the New Year party given by the Vincys, Farebrother notices that Lydgate is treated very coolly by his father-in-law and his wife. Very tactfully he offers help to the gloomy doctor, but it is refused.

Rather unexpectedly, Mrs Vincy is willing to invite Mary Garth to visit them again if Fred so desires it.

scientific phoenix Man of science who has sprung from nothing into a blaze of local glory. The remark is sarcastic.

systole and diastole in all inquiry The explanation of this medical metaphor is given in the statement that follows – 'a man's mind . . . object-glass'.

object-glass Magnifying glass.

tic-douloureux Spasmodic twitches of muscles caused by some nervous strain.

a Ken and a Tillotson Bishop Ken (1637–1711) and Archbishop Tillotson (1630–94) were both renowned for their high principles and convincing preaching.

Chapter 64

Lydgate now needs £1,000 to clear his pressing debts. His demands for economy are met by cold antagonism and accusations by Rosamond, who considers him entirely to blame for the situation.

He suggests that they sell the house to Ned Plymdale, a former suitor of hers who is getting married, and that they move to a smaller one. Rosamond is incensed by this, and again advocates moving from Middlemarch. At last he rounds on her and orders her to accept his decisions.

She is determined to obstruct his plans; therefore next day

she visits Mrs Plymdale to learn more of the forthcoming wedding, and finds an opportunity to say that she knows of no suitable house for sale. She then calls on Trumbull the auctioneer to cancel any arrangements made by her husband, and finishes her round of troublemaking by telling her husband that Plymdale has already found a suitable house.

When, on the following day, she admits to having cancelled the projected sale of their house, Lydgate is furious; they indulge in mutual recriminations with such heat that Rosamond is completely alienated from her husband. He is driven to considering the possibility of obtaining money from Sir Godwin; what he does not know is that his wife has already written to that rich relation and begged for assistance.

The shallowness ... becomes didactic A beautiful woman may be charming despite her empty-headedness until she attempts to tell a sensible man what to do.

Chapter 65

Sir Godwin writes to Lydgate; not only will he not help, but he expresses contempt for a man who lets his wife do the begging. Once again, Lydgate realizes, Rosamond has callously opposed him in secret; and, of course, he himself cannot now approach his relations. She has no understanding whatsoever of the wrongs she committed, and he has to admit defeat: he cannot communicate with her in any way.

Chapter 66

Though he is not a gambler by nature, Lydgate decides to try his hand. He calls in at the Green Dragon to see the dealer about selling his remaining horse, and begins to play billiards for money.

Fred Vincy drops in, seeking relaxation while Mary is away, and hoping to make a little towards paying off *his* debts. But young Hawley also arrives, and he is a very good billiards player. Soon he is taking away Lydgate's winnings. Fred realizes what is bound to happen, but cannot think of any way to get Lydgate from the table.

The next visitor is the Rector. Although he knows that he himself may benefit if Fred slides back into his dissolute habits, he resists temptation and makes every effort to end Fred's foolishness, which will greatly lower him in Mary's estimation.

twice-blessed mercy In *The Merchant of Venice*, Shakespeare writes that mercy is twice blessed: 'It blesseth him that gives and him that takes'.

Hercules and Theseus They performed tasks far beyond the ability of normal men, just as Fred is doing – or so he claims.

Chapter 67

As a result of his gambling, Lydgate is £5 the poorer. He thinks of applying to Bulstrode, but delays because the banker is now showing less interest in the hospital and he had never approved of his protégé's marriage.

Then Bulstrode sends for him: he is going into semi-retirement and will therefore withdraw his support of the hospital, which will become amalgamated with an older institution. Lydgate argues that such a move will mean the end of his research, and also his salary. If there could be some delay, he tells Bulstrode, Dorothea might well take over the patronage of the hospital when she returns from her holiday in Yorkshire. At last he informs the banker of his financial troubles, but all he gets is advice to declare himself bankrupt.

Philistine An uncultured person.

Chapter 68

One must now go back to a time before Lydgate's visit to
his patron. During Bulstrode's temporary absence, Raffles
stays at his house; on his return, the banker tries to allay
his wife's fears and confines the visitor to his bedroom. Then
very early one morning, he personally conducts Raffles away
from Middlemarch and tells him he will send money
regularly, but only so long as Raffles causes no trouble.

Nevertheless, he feels no sense of security. Therefore he
decides to leave Middlemarch, though he puts off the move
as long as possible. Garth is appointed his agent, and
suggests that the Stone Court estate could be let and that
Fred might be put in charge with the intention of his
eventually buying the stock on it. Bulstrode agrees but only
because he wants Garth to be in charge of his affairs.

During all this period, Mrs Bulstrode has been distraught
with foreboding and she, certainly, does not want to leave
the district. She, too, has heard of Lydgate's difficulties and
begs her husband to offer assistance.

Chapter 69

Garth finds Raffles very ill on the road and takes him into
Stone Court which is near. He then informs Bulstrode, who
sends to the hospital for Lydgate. Because of what he has
grasped from Raffles's delirious speech, Garth knows something of the secret and therefore not only resigns his own
position under Bulstrode but withdraws the scheme for Fred's
management.

The banker goes off to Stone Court, for he cannot trust
Raffles in his disturbed mental state. Lydgate diagnoses the
trouble as alcoholic poisoning and advocates rest and no
liquor. He is impressed by Bulstrode's apparent devotion
and tenderness in staying to nurse the invalid.

Having left Stone Court, Lydgate considers how, once the

house is sold, there will be nothing left by which to retain Rosamond's affection. He reaches home to find the bailiffs already in possession. The Vincys, outraged at this humiliation, have urged their daughter to return to the family home, and she has agreed.

toll-house The place where travellers paid to use a well-made turnpike road.

such large blue-bottles These large flies which throng round dirt symbolize relations who collect whenever there is a chance of receiving legacies.

Dr Ware John Ware's *History and Treatment of Delirium Tremens* was published in the USA in 1831; therefore Lydgate is not likely to have heard of it.

I may get my neck broken A condition of his marriage was that he should insure himself; therefore, if he meets with a fatal accident his wife will benefit financially.

Chapter 70

On going through Raffles's pockets, Bulstrode finds that he has been to Bilkley, but at the time the information suggests no threat to his security.

He stays with the sick man, fearful of what he may say in his delirium and trying to argue with himself that the blackmailer's death is justified. He now regrets having dismissed Lydgate from his post and so lost an ally.

When Lydgate calls, the patient is worse; he orders opium for a limited period and again forbids alcohol. Then Bulstrode asks him why he looks so worried, and, on hearing of the seizure of the furniture, offers a long-term loan of £1,000. Lydgate's joy is unbounded.

Too tired to stay with Raffles any longer, Bulstrode leaves him with Mrs Abel the housekeeper, but later returns, intending to tell her of the doctor's instructions about the opium, for he had genuinely forgotten to inform her. Yet he remains silent when she tells him that Raffles will take nothing but the drug; and when she recommends drinks of brandy, he gives her the key to the supply.

Next morning, Raffles is in a coma, but Bulstrode does not call Lydgate, and when the doctor eventually comes he can do nothing to save the patient. Nor is he in any position to question the circumstances of his death.

Farebrother calls on Lydgate to offer what help he can, and is told the wonderful news of the loan. He is far from happy, because he had already warned his friend against becoming involved with Bulstrode; and Lydgate himself feels that the money must have been offered for some purely selfish reason. Nonetheless, he is full of plans about how to begin anew.

news in the *Times* i.e. of the successful progress of the Reform Bill.

Chapter 71

Bambridge has been to Bilkley and there met a man who boasted of the hold he had on Bulstrode. Soon gossip races through Middlemarch of how the banker originally obtained his fortune, and in what way Ladislaw is connected with him. Farebrother immediately realizes what will be the implications of Lydgate attending Raffles at Stone Court and then receiving a huge 'loan'. The local doctors decide that there is insufficient evidence to warrant prosecution but Lydgate is more discredited than ever.

Bulstrode decides he had better take a short holiday; but he will not leave Middlemarch for good, and he intends to remain a man of public importance. With Lydgate he goes off to the Town Hall where there is a meeting to consider plans for a new burial ground. Before Bulstrode can speak, Hawley demands his retirement from Middlemarch affairs unless he can make a complete denial of the scandal. His reply is unconvincing: all he can say is that his accusers have made money in dubious ways and spent it on themselves whereas he has always used his wealth in the furtherance of good works. When the chairman orders him to leave the meeting, he goes in a state of collapse, aided by Lydgate, who thus seems to prove his close alliance with the disgraced banker.

Dorothea now returns from her holiday, eager to meet Lydgate and Bulstrode in order to arrange financial help for the hospital. She refuses to believe that the doctor has been guilty of any dishonourable act.

rising four Nearly four years old.
break Framework by which to train horses to draw a carriage.
Botany Bay The convict settlement in New South Wales.
he'd brag ... money He is such a boaster that he would praise a horse's faults as if he could gain a higher price by doing so.
as if it had been scored As certainly as if it was a debt chalked up as a constant reminder to the landlord.
turned his coat ... Romans Completely changed his political views and sided with the Roman Catholics. See Political Background, p.15.
Old Harry The Devil.
men at the tread-mill i.e. convicts.

Revision questions on Book Seven, Chapters 63–71

1 How is Rosamond's character illustrated by her attitude towards the debts which she and Lydgate have accumulated?

2 Explain how Bulstrode is affected by the revelation of the past.

3 What impression of Middlemarch people do you obtain from their reception of the news about Bulstrode, Lydgate, and the events of the former's past life?

4 To what extent do you sympathize with Lydgate because of the difficulties caused by his connection with Bulstrode?

5 Explain the moral dilemma confronting Bulstrode when Raffles is ill at Stone Court.

6 What is gained or lost by allowing Dorothea, Mary and Fred to take relatively little part in Book Seven?

Book Eight Sunset and Sunrise

Chapter 72

Dorothea is eager to help clear Lydgate's reputation, but Sir James, Celia and Farebrother are against her interference. She is overwhelmed by a sense of frustration.

Nemesis Retribution for one's sins.

Chapter 73

Having taken Bulstrode home, Lydgate rides off to consider the situation. He suspects the banker of having brought on Raffles's death, and wonders whether his own reactions would have been different if he had not received the £1,000. He knows he is ruined, but he determines to face the scandal and acknowledge his gratitude to Bulstrode. His chief worry is Rosamond's behaviour when she learns the full nature of the calamity.

he had denounced ... moral doubt He had objected most strongly to the way some people allow doubt about the truth of a scientific fact to become confused with their ideas of what is morally right or wrong.

Chapter 74

There is considerable sympathy in the town for Rosamond and Mrs Bulstrode; the latter has always been liked. Probably she has not heard the gossip for she has stayed indoors with her husband who is supposedly ill. When she questions Lydgate, she is not satisfied by his ambiguous replies; therefore she visits a number of acquaintances who only make matters vaguer and more ominous. Learning the truth from her brother, Mr Vincy, she returns home, locks herself in her room while she calms her mind about Bulstrode's years of deceit, and then, with all her finery removed, goes to offer him silent compassion and forgiveness.

low kind of religion Not only Low Church, but a religion followed by vulgar people.
methodistical Not necessarily belonging to the Methodist Church, but rather belonging to the Low Church of Nonconformists and making a display of their piety. Such behaviour would long be associated with the disgraced Bulstrode.
fit for Newgate Newgate prison, i.e. deserving to be hanged.
like an early Methodist i.e. very plain in dress.

Chapter 75

Despite being saved from the humiliation of debt, Rosamond is a very disgruntled woman: she sees no reason for economy, she wants to live in London, she is annoyed that Ladislaw has left Middlemarch and apparently prefers another woman, and she is disillusioned about her husband's rich relatives. She knows nothing of what happened in the Town Hall, and one day Lydgate finds her sending out invitations to a party; some have already been refused, and he furiously insists on her cancelling the project. To find out what lies behind his anger, Rosamond visits the Vincys; the information they give her is the heaviest blow she has ever received. On her return home she makes no attempt to sympathize, or even to tell Lydgate that she knows all; a resentful silence falls between them, and it is she who expects to receive pity. His efforts to make her understand the situation have no effect, and her only suggestion is that they move to London. Her behaviour is altogether too much for him, and he leaves the room ready to explode.

Earlier, Ladislaw had written saying that he might visit Middlemarch, and therefore Rosamond determines to tell him everything about her domestic situation, for she needs 'some one who would recognize her wrongs'.

Chapter 76

Lydgate is summoned to Lowick Manor, for Dorothea wants to ask him whether he will stay on at the hospital if she assures him of her belief in his integrity; she asks him for the full story of his connection with Raffles so that she may pass it on to other people. For the first time he receives genuine sympathy.

He tells her, in confidence, he has discovered that Raffles was given brandy and opium but he cannot be sure of the part played by Bulstrode; as both remedies are frequently prescribed for Raffles's ailment by less enlightened doctors, nobody can ascribe sinister motives to him.

Dorothea suggests he stays on at Middlemarch and gradually lives down the scandal; as she has money to spare, she is prepared to finance both him and the hospital. But Lydgate tells her he must not pain his wife too much and will therefore move to London; besides, in the circumstances it would be better to amalgamate the hospital with the older infirmary. In the course of the conversation Dorothea comes to understand something of the situation between him and his wife, and asks permission to visit her.

He leaves after refusing her loan, but immediately afterwards she writes begging to take over his debt and enclosing a cheque for £1,000. She decides to take the letter when she calls on Rosamond next day.

Louis and Laennec See notes pp.99 and 122.
get myself puffed Get the reputation of being a good doctor by people gossiping about me.

Chapter 77

Rosamond stays at home moping but is about to post a letter to Ladislaw urging him to visit her soon.

Dorothea is convinced that all Ladislaw's affections are centred on her, though she has no thoughts of remarriage. She sets off to visit Rosamond to tell her that Farebrother and she gladly accept Lydgate's version of the events at Stone Court. A flustered servant ushers her unannounced into the drawing-room, not knowing that her mistress is even in the house. Dorothea sees Ladislaw apparently fervently holding the hands of a tearful and sentimental Rosamond. After a few words, she departs, leaving the letter containing the cheque.

Now she sees Lydgate's domestic worries in a new light and is all the more resolved to clear his name; with a sort of feverish haste she drives off to tell Sir James and Mr Brooke the truth about the doctor and Bulstrode.

Hamlet-like raving Dorothea's mention of troubles reminds Celia of Hamlet's 'sea of troubles' against which he considered he might 'take arms', i.e. evolve some scheme for ending them.

Chapter 78

At Dorothea's departure, Ladislaw and Rosamond stand petrified. 'Don't touch me!' he shouts. His anger is terrible, for he sees no means of explaining the truth to Dorothea. He openly declares his love for Dorothea, and Rosamond is more pained than she had ever been by Lydgate's words or deeds. Ladislaw realizes, too, that as Rosamond had turned to him in her misery he may have become thoroughly compromised.

After he has gone, Rosamond collapses unconscious upon her bed. On his return, Lydgate tries unavailingly to comfort her, and assumes that the hysterical outburst has been caused by Dorothea's would-be helpful visit.

Chapter 79

When he comes downstairs, Lydgate finds Dorothea's letter. Then Ladislaw returns; obviously Lydgate does not know of his earlier call, and the servant did not; therefore he himself makes no reference to it.

For the first time Ladislaw hears that he is being connected with the scandal of Bulstrode's early career; to increase his embarrassment, he realizes he is being drawn into the shabby unhappiness of Lydgate and Rosamond, especially as they expect to continue their friendship in London.

Chapter 80

Dorothea goes to dine with the Farebrothers; when Ladislaw's name crops up in conversation she is so upset that she hurriedly leaves and cannot sleep for her grief. To the reader she reveals her love, mingled with anger, reproach and jealousy.

She falls asleep on the floor and, when she awakens, determines to dispel her sorrow by doing good to others. Lydgate is the one who most needs help; she deliberately puts on half-mourning to signify that a period of her life has ended, and sets off to see Rosamond.

all of a mummy Soft as pulp.

White of Selborne Gilbert White (1720–93) wrote about birds, animals and plants of the village of Selborne.

as sacred animals i.e. they could walk where they wished without interference from anyone, for they were sacred to some religion.

a mother ... by the sword The reference is to the judgement of Solomon recounted in I Kings 3, 16–28.

mater dolorosa The picture of Mary sorrowing for Christ.

plain quilling Decoration by a simple band of muslin or lace folded over at the edge.

ROSAMOND + DOROTHEA

Chapter 81

She finds Lydgate at home; he has decided to accept her cheque. Rosamond is loath to meet her, for she is uncertain of the reason for the visit. Dorothea offers heartfelt sympathy and says she has come to clear Lydgate's reputation. At this Rosamond collapses with relief and hysteria; soon her visitor too is nearly in tears. When Dorothea tries to explain the need for loyalty within marriage and the devastating effects of illicit affection, Rosamond holds her close and reveals the true nature of Ladislaw's visit. Eventually she and Lydgate are reconciled, though an air of sadness hangs over both.

Chapter 82

Ladislaw has yearned for an excuse to revisit Middlemarch, and now he decides to ask Bulstrode for the money rightly his so that he may finance a settlement in the Far West.

However, after the calamitous visit to Rosamond mentioned in Chapter 77 he goes away for the day. Yet so important is his friendship with the Lydgates that he returns to their house; during their tea-time meeting Rosamond treats him with coldness and puts into his saucer a note stating that she has told Dorothea of what really happened between them.

The Rubicon This refers to the phrase 'crossing the Rubicon', meaning to take an irrevocable step: the river itself was very small but under the Roman republic it was the boundary between Italy and Cisalpine Gaul; in 49 BC Caesar led his army across it into Italy, against the orders of the Senate, thereby declaring war on Pompey.

Chapter 83

To still her restlessness, Dorothea is studying ways of doing good. One day, Miss Noble, Farebrother's aunt, calls to ask if Ladislaw may visit Lowick Manor.

When he arrives it is to tell her the facts of his parentage and the purpose to which he intends putting Bulstrode's money; he confesses that all he cares for is her good opinion of him. As a storm brews up outside, Ladislaw at last tells her of his love, but renounces it because he is poor; it is Dorothea who insists that they can marry some day, for she detests her wealth and they can well live on her own £700 p.a. At last they understand each other's feelings.

had flannel The distribution of lengths of flannel to the poor was a favourite method of being charitable.
mere pen and a mouthpiece i.e. a journalist who merely puts into writing the opinions of a political group without himself believing in them.

Chapter 84

At Freshitt Hall Brooke announces that Dorothea is to marry Ladislaw; Sir James is infuriated at the supposed disgrace to the family, though he admits to himself that he feels mortified because the Freshitt and Tipton estates will not become amalgamated as he had hoped. He blames Brooke for encouraging Ladislaw to remain in Middlemarch, and refuses to have anything to do with Dorothea's husband. Plainly believing that her sister is very selfish, Celia goes off to tell Dorothea of the family's views, but her complaints are brushed aside. There need be no embarrassment, for Ladislaw and his wife intend to live in London.

a Draco, a Jeffreys Draco of Athens (*c*. 600 BC) and Lord Jeffreys (1644–89) were very severe judges.
free from humours Suffering from no emotional strain.

Chapter 85

Distressed by his wife's sufferings, Bulstrode is preparing to leave Middlemarch and to arrange for the management of Stone Court, which he is bequeathing to his wife.

  She wants him to help Rosamond and Lydgate but he has to confess that his loan has been returned. This further proof of isolation from society overcomes her; therefore he suggests that she approach Garth about managing the estate and establishing Fred Vincy on it.

Bunyan John Bunyan (1628–88) tells, in *The Pilgrim's Progress*, how the personified sins and weaknesses of humanity acted as witnesses and jury in condemning Faithful to death.

Chapter 86

Garth enjoys teasing Mary about his wonderful news, but when it is learnt that Fred will be in charge of the Stone Court land and can eventually buy the stock on it, she agrees to marry him without delay.

Finale

Although Fred never grows rich, he makes a success of estate management, and his gratitude to Farebrother is always acknowledged.

Lydgate builds up an excellent practice in London and Germany, but he considers himself a failure. Rosamond stays faithful but stubbornly selfish; when her husband dies at the age of fifty, she is glad to begin a new and easier life married to an elderly but wealthy physician.

Dorothea and Ladislaw are happy in their marriage, and his interest in politics eventually results in his being elected to Parliament. Brooke invites them to the Grange where he tells them that arrangements for the future of his estate have not been altered, as he had once threatened, and therefore in time it will pass into the possession of their son.

News of this son's birth excites Celia. She insists on going to see Dorothea, and Sir James is almost as eager to take her. The families meet and are reconciled, although Sir James is always very formal in his attitude towards Ladislaw.

round jacket Waist-length jacket worn by young boys.
basil plant This and the murdered man's brains are references to *Isabella*, a poem by John Keats.
Municipal Reform See Political Background, p.14.
entail The settlement of land on one's successors under certain conditions.
that river ... the strength Cyrus the Great of Persia dispersed the river Gyndes into numerous shallow channels because it had barred his progress.

Revision questions on Book Eight, Chapter 72–Finale

1 Do you consider that the story of Lydgate and Rosamond comes to a satisfactory or unsatisfactory conclusion? For what reasons?

2 Give a description of Mrs Bulstrode's state of mind and activities during the period of her grief and disillusion.

3 Explain how Bulstrode attempted to do some good as atonement for his past misconduct. To what extent do you believe he was sincere?

4 Analyse carefully Dorothea's relations with Rosamond in this part of the novel.

5 For what reasons would you claim that Ladislaw deserves the happiness he eventually enjoys?

6 'The story of Fred and Mary is brought to a hasty and perfunctory conclusion.' How far would you agree with this statement?

General questions

1 For what reasons, in your opinion, did Dorothea marry Casaubon rather than Chettam?

2 Explain carefully the main reasons for the breakdown of Casaubon's relationship with Dorothea.

3 'A most unpleasant family.' How far would you agree with this description of Mr and Mrs Vincy, Fred and Rosamond?

4 Give a brief and clear account of the events connected with the New Hospital.

5 Give an account of how Featherstone attempted to rule the lives of people while he was sick and also when he was dead.

6 Both Lydgate and the young Bulstrode felt the need to make money and succeed in their careers. Show clearly how they attempted to achieve their ambitions.

7 Explain how lack of money affects the lives of Ladislaw, and of Fred Vincy.

8 Give an account of Casaubon's stay in Rome so as to illustrate important aspects of his character.

9 To what extent do you find Raffles a person whose character and actions seem true to life?

10 Give an account of Rosamond's reaction to her husband's debts, and give your opinion of her attitude.

11 What is the purpose of introducing the 'lower-class' characters of both town and country, especially as they appear so little?

12 What part does Mr Farebrother play in the novel? What is your opinion of his attitude towards Mary?

13 To what extent is Celia a satisfactory contrast with her sister Dorothea?

14 Bring out the two different sides to Ladislaw's character by describing him in Rome, and then engaged in politics at Middlemarch.

15 Give an account of how Fred changed into a responsible and quite industrious young man.

16 Give an account of Rosamond's interest in and flirtations with men other than her husband.

17 Show how Dorothea, Caleb Garth and Mr Brooke do good to others in different ways and for different reasons.

18 For what reasons do you consider that Bulstrode was unpopular in Middlemarch *before* people knew of his early life?

19 Write character-sketches of two of the following: Borthrop Trumbull, Mrs Cadwallader, Joshua Rigg, Mrs Waule.

20 Which of the women in *Middlemarch* best illustrates the desire to achieve something despite the circumstances in which she lives? Give your reasons.

21 Refer to details in the novel in order to explain the *social* position of doctors in Middlemarch. You should not confine yourself to Lydgate.

22 From *Middlemarch* illustrate the life of the landed gentry of the times, making clear what they considered to be the duties and responsibilities owed to them and by them.

23 For what reasons, in your opinion, did George Eliot make religion and clergymen important to her novel?

24 Give an account of the movement for Parliamentary Reform as described in *Middlemarch*.

25 Show in some detail how George Eliot introduces into Book One subject matter which is important to later developments of the story.

26 Which episode to you consider to be of greatest importance in the development of the Ladislaw-Casaubon-Dorothea story? Write a short account of it and give your reasons for considering it important.

27 'The novel depends too much on coincidence.' Do you consider this to be a fair judgement of *Middlemarch*?

28 For what reasons did Lydgate's marriage fail? You should bear in mind that he himself was partly responsible.

29 What can be said to support the suggestion that the most successful marriage would have been one between Lydgate and Dorothea?

30 By reference to events in the novel, show that the inhabitants of Middlemarch are always highly suspicious of anyone not born and bred there.